BBC TopGear

HYPERCARS

THE GREATEST AUTOMOTIVE GAMECHANGERS

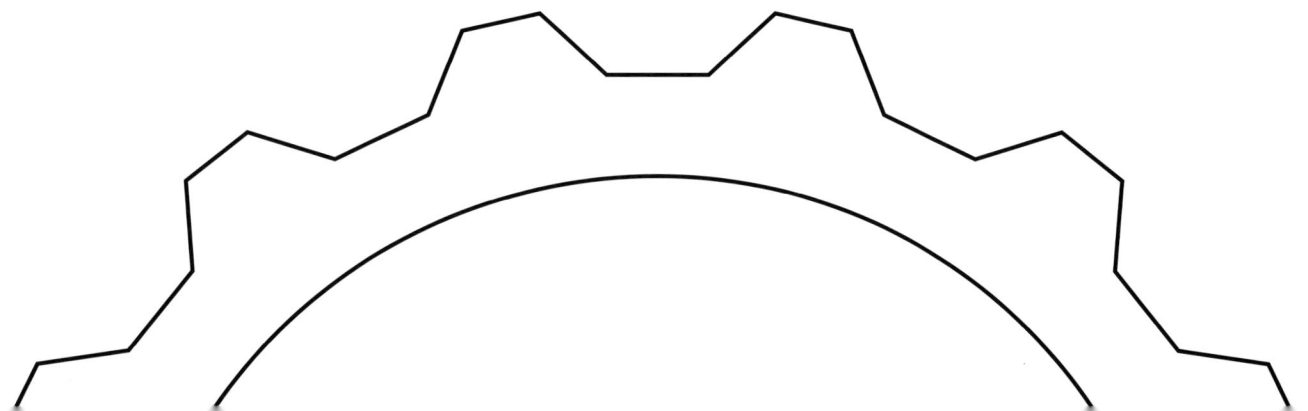

BBC TopGear

HYPERCARS

THE GREATEST AUTOMOTIVE GAMECHANGERS

Jason Barlow

BBC BOOKS

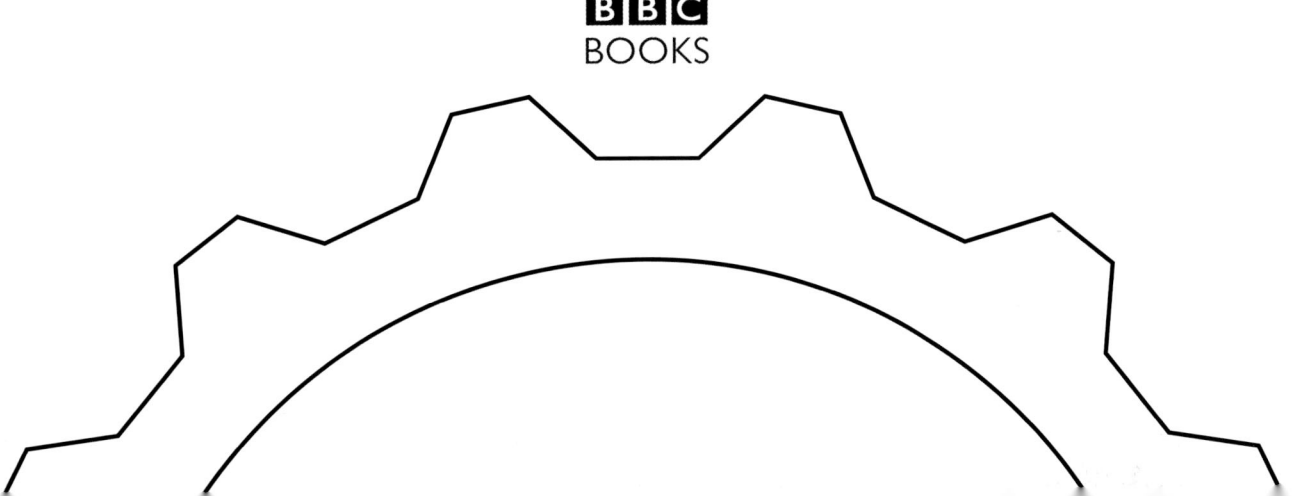

CONTENTS

FOREWORD p.6

IN THE BEGINNING p.8

1 ALFA ROMEO 33 STRADALE p.20

2 ASTON MARTIN VALKYRIE p.34

3 BUGATTI TOURBILLON p.50

4 CZINGER 21C p.66

5 FERRARI DAYTONA SP3 p.82

6 GMA T.50 p.98

7 KOENIGSEGG JESKO ABSOLUT p.116

8 LAMBORGHINI COUNTACH LPI 800-4 p.132

9 LAMBORGHINI REVUELTO p.148

10 LOTUS EVIJA p.164

11 McLAREN SPEEDTAIL p.180

12 MERCEDES AMG ONE p.196

13 PAGANI UTOPIA p.212

14 RED BULL RB17 p.228

15 RIMAC NEVERA p.246

CREDITS p.262

FOREWORD

HORACIO PAGANI
CEO and founder, Pagani

Two of the most defining characteristics of a Hypercar are performance and aesthetics. Both guide our creative process at Pagani. When you think about performance you have to look at racing cars, and one thing they all have in common is a focus on weight reduction and guaranteeing safety. Naturally I want to find that in a Hypercar as well. Additionally, a Hypercar must exude beauty and evoke an emotional response from its driver. It must be unique and possess great personality and energy, generating a desire strong enough that someone would be willing to spend millions on what is a useless object if thought of merely as a means of getting from A to B!

These are interesting times in the automotive world, but our clients have consistently expressed a preference for analogue driving experiences, characterised by the visceral sensation of a V12 engine. This is the ultimate expression of mechanical engineering, and a V12 nowadays is comparable to a Tourbillon in a fine Swiss wristwatch. Despite the potential for higher power with alternative powertrains, as seen in V8 hybrids and electric cars, our customers prioritise the emotion and engagement offered by traditional combustion engines. Speed and acceleration, while important, are secondary considerations for those who invest in Pagani vehicles.

Leonardo da Vinci taught us over 500 years ago that art and science are disciplines that can walk together hand-in-hand. Considering how much Hypercars cost, there is no doubt that they must contain state-of-the-art technology. That said, the Pagani customer is more attuned to the overall experience, the feeling that you are engaging whilst driving the car or even just looking at it in the garage. The Zonda is now 25 years old, and as Pagani's inaugural model it put our name on the map and won the hearts of a certain type of clientele. In some ways this is the car that invented the Hypercar segment because it was extremely provocative, different in its proportions to anything else out there. There are only 140 road-going Zondas worldwide, a small proportion considering the size of the global market. This scarcity, together with the Zonda's characteristics, has resulted in the residual values of some Zondas reaching 20 times their original cost. Our wish is for our new Utopia model to prompt similar levels of devotion and admiration.

First there was the supercar. The hypercar was the next evolutionary step. This is the story of the greatest automotive adventure of them all

IN THE BEGINNING

It's unquestionably one of those days. We're on an airfield in Germany with a McLaren F1 and Bugatti Veyron. You need an empty runway to fully appreciate what are arguably the two most significant high performance cars ever made. The former, we reckon, marks the point at which the supercar stepped up and morphed into the hypercar. Why? Because the F1's carbon fibre construction, exclusivity, aerodynamics, and race-bred 6.1-litre V12 engine were all next-level. It was conceived by motorsport tech genius Gordon Murray, and the word 'supercar' suddenly just didn't seem sufficient.

And what of the Veyron? It was a car born of a vast technological struggle, that required colossal effort and expense on the part of Bugatti's parent company, Volkswagen. Its engine was a mammoth eight litres in capacity, fed by 16 cylinders and boosted by four turbochargers to deliver a power output of 1,001PS (987bhp). Yet it was designed to be no more challenging to use on a daily basis than a humble Volkswagen Polo.

Crucially, it also bore the imprimatur of a big name and was willed into existence by the late Ferdinand Piëch; personality and ego being two further key components in the evolution of the hypercar. Scion of the Porsche family, Piëch announced his arrival as a major force when he masterminded the formidable Porsche 917 endurance racer, in the late Sixties. He would later steer Audi towards greatness (the ground-breaking Quattro was done under his watch in the late Seventies), before ultimately assuming command of the entire VW empire in the Nineties. A collector and curator of brands, Piëch bought Bugatti in 1998 (adding it to a trophy cabinet that already included Bentley and Lamborghini). Capping a stellar career, the Veyron was to be his ultimate statement of intent.

These two titans chased similar goals but were philosophically opposed. This added fascination to an already gripping story. Professor Gordon Murray, a former Formula One technical director, espoused light weight above all else. He was (still is) an ingeniously left-field thinker. At the Brabham team in the late Seventies, he'd devised the famous – infamous even – BT46B "fan car", which was too clever for its own good and was withdrawn from competition. Driven by a purity of approach, Murray claimed and still claims to be disinterested in zero to 62mph times or top speeds, two of the parameters by which we judge a hypercar. For him, they're a byproduct of a car's engineering, not its reason for being.

This didn't stop the F1 road car from being seismic, though. A plan was hatched late in 1988, and once team boss Ron Dennis and his fellow McLaren executives had agreed to proceed, Murray wrote a product plan on four sides of A4. It was a typically focused manifesto. "No compromise, no plastic, three seat layout, use F1 technology to create ground effect, automatic retractable aero devices, composite monocoque and body, survival cell à la F1, F1 engine, six-speed transaxle, carbon clutch, electronic differential, 200mph-plus top speed, more than 1g in lateral acceleration, F1 push- or pull-rod suspension, carbon brakes, gearchange and steering position to suit buyer…"

An overtaking button was also considered, and despite his adherence to engineering and aero first principles, Murray knew full well the value of marketing. The F1, he noted, was "all about mystique… the product should sell itself." The car would also have a maximum weight of 1,000kg, would be no more than 1.8 metres wide, and its front and rear overhangs would be minimal. "Aerodynamically we had to maintain the centre of pressure position, something production car manufacturers never addressed and which accounts for high speed instability," he remembered some years later.

The McLaren F1 was defined as much by what it didn't have as by what it did. Traction control and ABS were notable omissions, a punchy decision even by early Nineties standards. Then there was its central driving position, a key USP and proof that clever packaging was as important – and crowd-pleasing – as a powerful, charismatic engine. Mind you, there was room for a passenger on either side and space for their luggage. Great credit is also due to Peter Stevens, the quietly influential and ultra-intuitive designer who gave the McLaren F1 its timeless form, though it's Murray who remains the auteur.

"If you want to do a pure, focused driver's car, it has to be a single person car, not a committee. Whether it's styling, packaging… you will never

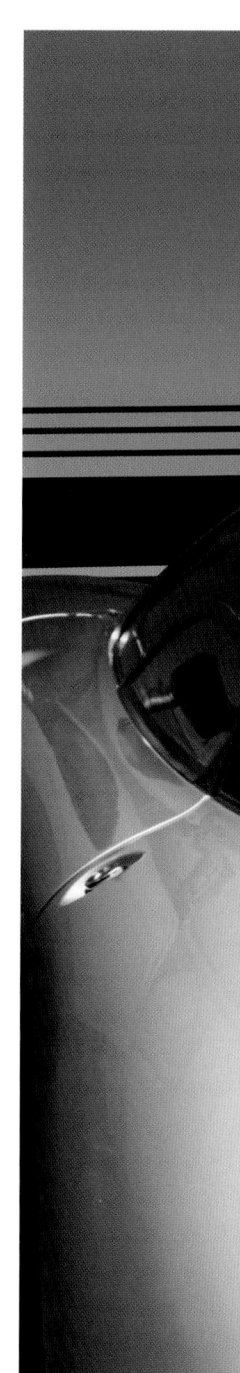

The McLaren F1 is the Year Zero for the hypercar, and not just because it uses gold foil in its engine bay to deflect the heat generated by a 6.1-litre, motorsport-inspired V12. This car is also a pure Vision Thing

get pure focus if you have more than one person leading a team," he told me in a 2019 interview. "You also need a genuinely clean sheet of paper. McLaren, Ferrari, Pagani – they've got existing powertrains and chassis, so of course they're going to make the next model using those. It's the right thing to do economically."

He continues: "On the F1, everything was drawn from scratch, and how many cars can you say that about? The Aston Martin Valkyrie? It's a racing car for the road. The Veyron was a clean sheet project, but it was also done by a massive committee, one that changed several times during its development. There's a huge giggle factor of having 1,000bhp, then booting it out of a second gear corner and trying to hold on. But I hated the turbo lag it had on the road."

Even with four turbos, the Veyron definitely still feels like a car with forced induction. For many, that huge rush as the boost builds is a big part of the car's appeal. Bugatti gloried in the Veyron's 252mph terminal velocity, although its ease of use elsewhere is just as impressive. The company maximised on this characteristic when it developed the Chiron, and indeed on the car that followed it, the incredible new Tourbillon.

Back on our German airfield, it's time to meet another big personality, a human one this time. Andy Wallace is in full effect. A Le Mans and multiple Daytona 24 Hours winner, this disarmingly humble Briton has lately become a key figure in the hypercar sphere. In 1998, he set a new world speed record of 240.1mph in a McLaren F1, proving the car's credentials despite Murray's disdain. He did it again in 2019, this time behind the wheel of a Bugatti Chiron Super Sport, hitting a V-Max of 304.8mph at the VW group's Ehra-Lessien test track. This is one of the few places in the world with a straight long enough to attempt such a feat, and Wallace is one of the few people brave enough to try. He has plenty of stories to tell.

"When you talk about the McLaren F1, it was such a different time," he recalls with a smile. "Even though the actual horsepower number wasn't crazy mad, it was a crazy mad car, so it definitely deserves its place if you're talking about the evolution of the hypercar. I guess it was the one that really started everything off. Mind you, your reactions needed to be razor sharp if you got a certain amount out of shape in one…"

This raises an important point: although it should be brilliantly engineered, a hypercar should also challenge the driver. Those early supercars – Seventies machines such as the Ferrari 512 BB, Lamborghini Countach and Porsche Turbo – all had a reputation for not suffering fools gladly. Hypercars demand respect, and the latest generation underlines that. Wallace tells a good story about the F1 during its fabled record run.

"It became unstable and I noticed it was moving around quite a bit. This was around the 230mph mark," he says with amusing understatement. "If you lifted off at that point, well, that's as fast as you're ever going to go. But if you kept your foot in, you could get through that and come out the

"THE CENTRAL DRIVING POSITION IS ONE OF THE McLAREN F1'S KEY FEATURES. THE VIEW OUT IS PERFECT"

other side. You can gather lots of information from large-scale wind tunnel models, but it's difficult to predict everything. Gordon suspected it was some kind of vortex acting on the car, and because I was still racing a lot at the time, I figured I could deal with it. So I did. My imagination was a lot smaller back then. You think you're almost invincible."

More than 20 years later, as we noted, he was record-breaking again, demonstrating that the Bugatti Chiron – in an aerodynamically optimised and elongated Super Sport guise – represented another paradigm shift in the hypercar story. If exclusivity and engineering superiority are two hallmarks of a hypercar, then breaking barriers is another. How does 300mph grab you?

Wallace and the team behind the Bugatti record had their work cut out. "It's different in every car. Obviously, much depends on aerodynamics," he explains. "But it also depends on things like chassis stiffness. If you've got an engine with an awful lot of torque, and it's obviously trying to twist the chassis, it's encouraging if the car is very resistant to that. If you take a corner when you're driving a car very quickly, you feel really calm if what happens next is what you expected to happen. You feel under control. This is obviously a good thing."

The Chiron is a paragon of control. Not that the Super Sport's record run went completely to plan. Somewhere above 280mph, the wheels were turning so fast that they overwhelmed the car's front suspension geometry. "I was aware that if I put a small input in to correct the trajectory, because the wind blew the car off course ever so slightly, it wasn't a case of, 'input, car settles, relax'," Wallace recalls. "No, I then had to put another input in to counter the first one." Basically, the car wanted to keep on turning.

Now imagine doing this at 280mph-plus. The engineers checked the tyres – each one of which was being battered by a force equivalent to seven tonnes that wanted to rip them to shreds – and fixed the steering issue. Wallace went back out, nailing the throttle as he exited one of the track's braked turns at 160mph. A ripple in the track surface caused the Chiron to jump briefly but it settled again instantly. Having broken the 300mph barrier – by a 4.7mph margin – the less soul-stirring, but no less dramatic, business of slowing the Bugatti down could begin. On the record run, the gantry he'd been using as a braking marker arrived sooner than it had done previously because he was travelling that much faster. Wallace, like all top-flight racing drivers, knows what 200mph, even 230mph, feels like. But 300 is like a trip into *The Twilight Zone*. The fact is, most things travelling at that speed are already airborne by this point. "Things happen *very* quickly at 300mph," Wallace says. "You could argue that it's not particularly relevant. But then the German car industry makes cars that can go very fast on the autobahn, and if a car is capable of 300mph, then how ridiculously easy is it to do 200? The Chiron is a car with brakes that can pull it up from 300. The engineering involved is incredible. There's a confidence here."

This is a concept to keep in mind. Ettore and Jean Bugatti had confidence in their immense project back when it all started in the Twenties and Thirties. Enzo Ferrari and Ferruccio Lamborghini were sustained by huge self-belief through good times and bad when they began manufacturing cars. The super- and hypercar is the stuff of dreams, and even as electrification arrives to change – and charge – things up yet again, still they come. In the decades since McLaren set the hypercar stage with the F1, a handful of new entrants have established themselves – armed with grit and determination, and without the backing of a wealthy corporate benefactor.

Pagani is perhaps the most prominent. Horacio Pagani was born in Argentina in 1955 and like many before him worked his way up the hard way. He read all he could about Leonardo da Vinci, but at the same time disassembled an old Renault Dauphine so he could turn it into a Dune Buggie (using a local company's kit). Aged 18, he enrolled in the university

"TOP RACING DRIVERS HAVE AN IDEA WHAT 230MPH FEELS LIKE. BUT 300 IS A TRIP INTO THE UNKNOWN..."

Extraordinarily well engineered and fabulous to look at, the Bugatti Chiron is also a car with an epic bandwidth

of La Plata, not far from Buenos Aires, studying industrial design. These were violent times in Argentina, so Pagani switched to mechanical engineering in the quieter city of Rosario. Then, to his parents' dismay, he abandoned his studies in favour of setting up an engineering workshop, whose sole employee was Horacio himself. Amongst other things, he manufactured agricultural tools and a custom hardtop for the family bakery's pick-up. His first commercially displayed project was a caravan, which had been converted for use as a mobile radio station. Having helped a local racing driver modify his car, Pagani was soon at work on a design of his own, and even at this early stage, and despite the obvious fiscal challenges, he was fastidious. And ingenious: the uprights on the rear spoiler were repurposed from a war plane he and his colleagues found in a scrapyard.

Later, he would meet the great Argentinian racing hero, Juan Manuel Fangio, who helped him draft letters to Italy's big names and set him on the path that would see him relocate to Europe. In Italy, he met Ferrari's engineering legend Mauro Forghieri, who told him that while Ferrari didn't need any designers, he would offer him a position at the Scuderia. Despite this, Pagani held out for a role at Lamborghini, a better place, he felt, from which to launch his campaign to "design the most beautiful car in the world". Lamborghini came through – eventually – but Pagani started as a third-level manual worker, the lowliest position, and he and his wife Crista lived for a time on a local campsite.

Having led Lamborghini's early foray into the brave new world of composites, he gained huge knowledge and expertise in an area that would come to define his own cars. He financed the purchase of an autoclave, and became a prime exponent of the material that revolutionised the hypercar: carbon fibre. Meanwhile, back in Woking, England, Gordon Murray was thinking along similar lines…

His old mentor Fangio introduced him to Mercedes engineering boss (and future CEO) Dieter Zetsche, who liked what he saw and pledged to support Pagani with powertrains. The man himself promised to stay true to his desire to create something powerful but light, not just designing but crafting all the componentry by hand. In so doing, he was keeping the faith with another idea, one whose roots lay in his childhood fascination with Da Vinci: to create a car that embodied the values of a latter-day Renaissance sculpture, one whose technical composition did not overwhelm its human

Above, the Bugatti Veyron is often said to be the Concorde of the car world. Left, the Ferrari F50, a car whose reputation grows with every passing year

Right, the Bugatti Chiron Super Sport, the 300mph-plus hypercar. Below, Andy Wallace, the former racing driver who took the Bugatti to the very edge of what is possible

attributes. Still, he had to battle external forces: in the wake of the Gulf War and the resulting economic uncertainties, the mid-Nineties were scarcely favourable to an unheard-of car maker. Codenamed the C8, the result was the Zonda, a machine of gloriously provocative, lightweight design (just 1,250kg), one that immediately ignited desire amongst its wealthy target demographic as well as demanding poster space on a million bedroom walls. With the driver positioned further forward than on rival cars, and seated purposefully in a cockpit, the Zonda's shape was equal parts fighter jet and Group C racer. Carbon fibre, of course, was used extensively and intelligently, for this was Pagani's calling card. Zetsche's pledge was honoured: power came from Mercedes-AMG's V12, initially a 6.0-litre, later bored out to seven litres with a 542bhp power output, and then 7.3 litres and eventually a peak of 789bhp.

Inside, Pagani's fiercely artisanal spirit was in full effect. The Zonda was almost steampunk in places, and yet somehow managed to be a classic Italian high performance car, tailored to fit with visible mechanical elements and meticulously wrought pedals. Although with its low scuttle height and cleverly designed glasshouse, it was easier to place on the road than most. Pagani talked of infusing the Zonda with the spirit of Fangio, an unusual claim that he fulfilled.

The Zonda was followed by the C9, otherwise known as the Huayra, the difficult second album. Its Mercedes-sourced 6.0-litre V12 was now twin-turbocharged though with Pagani-prescribed modifications in order to reduce lag. More classically pretty than the Zonda, the Huayra also featured active aerodynamics, a titanium exhaust, and would later be infused with a new, even lighter form of carbon fibre (called Carbo-Triax). Now, as the company celebrates its 25th anniversary, we welcome the third Pagani, the Utopia, named, as 16th century philosopher and Lord Chancellor Thomas More first posited it, in honour of an ideal place or perhaps state of mind. Interestingly, Pagani's clients prioritised simplicity, lightness, and the pleasure of driving when asked what mattered most. So no electrification or hybridisation here,

then, and no central touchscreen inside. The new car can even be ordered with a fully manual gearbox, despite its 864bhp power output and 811lb ft of torque. Intriguingly, this new Pagani suggests that perhaps we've had our Utopia. Now we just need to hang onto it. From 25 employees in 1999, Pagani now has 180. But it's still closer in spirit to a sculptor's workshop than a car maker.

Then there's Koenigsegg, perhaps the other great addition to the hypercar canon, and a company that also does things very much its own way. But this one is Swedish rather than headquartered in Italy's famous "motor valley". It operates out of hangars in a town called Ängelholm that were once occupied by a fighter pilot unit of the Swedish Air Force, buildings that have swapped one extreme for another. As with Ferrari, Lamborghini and Pagani, these are cars with big personalities brought to life by a visionary figure who's most definitely larger than life. Christian von Koenigsegg dreamt of making his own cars from childhood, and staked everything he had on making it happen. Like Pagani, there's a degree of artistry in what Koenigsegg does, in that it makes virtually all of its own components. Unsurprisingly, there's a similar doggedness to the story. Christian von Koenigsegg lived hand-to-mouth in the company's early Nineties infancy, until his father Jesko sold his own company and invested in his son's. Their farmhouse base burnt down in 2003, prompting the move to an abandoned airfield and the hangars they're still in. By riding the hypercar wave – and often dictating the direction of travel – the company has expanded to the point where Koenigsegg now employs 650 people, and has joined Abba, Ikea and Volvo amongst Sweden's most famous exports.

"What is the biggest contribution Koenigsegg is giving to society?" he asks us rhetorically. "We're supplying very few expensive cars to the wealthy car enthusiast, but we invent and create interesting technology that can trickle down. We show you can live your dream, show that stuff out of the ordinary is possible, and we lift spirits and make people believe."

This much is true, and von Koenigsegg is closer in spirit to an automotive Willy Wonka than he is a successor to Enzo Ferrari. Not least because he has completely reimagined almost every aspect of the high performance car. Why? It's quite simple, really. Because he wanted to.

The Regera has a twin turbo V8 and three electric motors to produce a little less than 1,800bhp but a "direct drive" to the rear axle replaces a conventional mechanism, and the car uses a single-speed gearbox. A particularly robust aluminium "HydraCoup" torque converter does the heavy lifting instead. Then there's that extraordinary transmission. Koenigsegg has also captured hearts and minds via increasingly flamboyant yet somehow rational exterior design, boosted by showstoppers such as the "dihedral synchro-helix doors" – the hinges move out and then up – and the so-called "autoskin" whose mechanisms allow all the moving exterior panels to operate hydraulically. Or how about the "Flex" sensor system that allows

"THE PAGANI ZONDA WAS EQUAL PARTS GROUP C RACER AND FIGHTER JET"

Koenigsegg's cars to run on E85 biofuel? This is all great left-field thinking.

You can read about the Jesko Absolut in this book, a car that Christian von Koenigsegg hopes might reclaim the record for the world's fastest production car from Bugatti. It might even become the first to break the 500km/h barrier (310mph), although he knows that chasing those sorts of speeds is only one part of the equation. "There is a price to pay for top speed, because everything else in the car has to cope. You have to bleed off your downforce, you have to have a certain type of tyre technology, suspension technology, gear ratios… it all adds weight."

Not everything since the early Nineties dawn of the hypercar has been about top speed; there are other barriers to break, different mountains to climb. Accordingly, the Aston Martin Valkryrie and Mercedes AMG One are two of the most fascinating cars ever made. Aston collaborated with the Red Bull F1 team in a valiant effort to create a road car that had the violent performance and aerodynamic profile of an extreme track car. Mercedes-AMG determined to take its all-conquering hybrid Formula One powertrain and fit it to a car that could be used on road and track. These projects tested their development teams to the limit. Red Bull, still smarting from the way the Valkyrie project concluded, elected to build its own track-only car, the £5m RB17. Adrian Newey may have matched Gordon Murray's achievements in Formula One, but can his long dreamt-of car move things forward as profoundly as the McLaren F1 did? Murray, meanwhile, has recently eclipsed himself with the GMA T.50, the car that exceeds the F1 for purity and aerodynamic efficiency and fixes the things on the original that always bugged its creator… Once again, however, Murray has gone his own way, disinclined to get tangled up in any 300mph shenanigans. A road car and track car are two very different things, although he has entered the fray here with the T.50s Niki Lauda. This is the even more limited production track-only iteration of the T.50, which weighs just 852kg and wrings another 50bhp from the Cosworth-supplied 4.0-litre V12, making a total power output of 700bhp. At high speeds the ram effect on the engine's air intake will increase that to 725bhp. In such a light car that equals fireworks.

And what of Ferrari, perhaps the greatest name of all in automotive? It started the track-only trend with the mighty FXX in 2005, and continues to inspire more devotion than any of its competitors. Indeed, in terms of brand it's in a different dimension, and one could argue that the Purosangue is almost a hyper-GT if not a hypercar in the sense we've defined it here. The F50 arrived in 1995 into a world whose expectations had been recalibrated by the McLaren F1, and despite its carbon fibre chassis and a 4.7-litre V12 directly related to the glorious 1990 641 Formula One car, the F50 was rather overlooked. That seems impossible to believe, looking back. History now records this as one of the great modern Ferraris, revered for its naturally aspirated engine and manual gearbox. And it's rare, too, with just 349 produced. Ferrari sees itself as a breed apart, but the F50, and the Enzo and LaFerrari that followed, are true hypercars. The next Ferrari hypercar, codenamed F250, is almost here, and promises to rearrange the parameters while setting some new ones. McLaren, too, is well represented in this book, the Speedtail representing a similar 'moon shot' ambition to the Mercedes AMG One and Aston Martin Valkyrie. With its outrageous elongated body and highly aerodynamic properties, it achieves a top speed of 250mph.

Just 250mph. As the hypercar inevitably tilts towards full electrification, we have to ask: where will it all end? The other great newcomer of the era is Rimac, whose story is perhaps the biggest fairytale of all. In 2008, Mate Rimac was setting world records in an old BMW 3 series he'd converted to an EV, using a powertrain of his own design. That same year, he was the sole employee of the newly founded Rimac Automobili. A decade later, he presented the C_2 at the Geneva Motor Show and Porsche took a 10 per cent stake in his company. The Nevera was launched in 2021, and fried minds with its huge performance. More even than that, it proved that an electric car could have the two most critical things for any hypercar, heart and soul.

Over to Mate for the final words, from a conversation chaired by *Top Gear* that also included Christian von Koenigsegg, American power-broker John Hennessey and Gordon Murray. "Nobody needs to go 300mph and nobody needs a hypercar, but life is not only about problems we need to solve to survive. I always say cars are the accumulation of human ingenuity and knowledge. You have everything there, material sciences, fluid dynamics, simulations, electronics, software. Plus, it's a piece of art. When a rally with 50 hypercars comes into a city, the city stops. There are tens of thousands of people on the roads, little kids touching these cars, taking photos, sitting in the car, being inspired by it. Which other product in the world can do that? What else can you put in front of people to cause that fascination?"

"CARS ARE THE ACCUMULATION OF HUMAN INGENUITY AND KNOWLEDGE. THEY'RE ALSO ART"

Left, somewhere in the midst of the tyre smoke is a Koenigsegg, the biggest thing to come out of Sweden since Ikea. Below, the Hennessey Venom F5 in its natural runway habitat

Hypercar summit: from left, John Hennessey, Mate Rimac, Gordon Murray and Christian von Koenigsegg meet The Stig

WHY IT'S HERE
We're pushing the definition of hypercar a bit but this is a £2m-plus limited edition Alfa Romeo, so what's not to love?

ALFA ROMEO 33 STRADALE

The Alfa Romeo 33 Stradale meets its famous 1967 forebear, a car whose body, roof and entire existence all flirted with the impossible. The new car is a similarly ambitious machine from a company determined to make good on its rich history

It's 11pm so it's night in Alfa Romeo's museum. There's scarcely another soul to be seen. This is quite the privilege and it prompts an important thought: these guys' hit rate is extraordinary. There's a pale blue late Thirties 8C 2900B Lungo, a TZ2, a classic Giulia Super in blue and sirened Carabinieri form (*pronto intervento*)… How cool is that? There are 70 cars on permanent display, all in all, with more treasure stashed away back-stage.

But this is a human story, too. Take Alfa's Sixties CEO Giuseppe Eugenio Luraghi, an engineer who also happened to be a poet, writer and polymath. Like so many Italian grandees of this period, his eyewear was on point, too. More importantly, it was he who decreed Alfa Romeo should go racing again. To which end he hired former Ferrari engineer and all-round genius Carlo Chiti to facilitate. The result was the 33 bloodline, a series of competition cars to rival the best that Ferrari and Porsche conjured up in that big-sunglasses-and-sidies golden era.

Teasing them all was the 33 Stradale, a road car designed by Franco Scaglione, the author of more great cars than there is space to list (check out the Alfa Romeo B.A.T cars and Lamborghini 350 GTV as a primer). But the 33 is his masterpiece, a car that retains its capacity to stun six decades later. Only 18 were made, and six were cannibalised to underpin some of the world's most influential concepts, including '68's seismic Marcello Gandini-designed Alfa Romeo Carabo.

Now meet the new 33 Stradale, a mid-engined *fuoriserie* (limited edition)

Left, the interior shuns modern touchscreens in favour of hand-made physical switchgear

Above and left, the main instrument display is digital but elsewhere the 33 Stradale is all about metal and leather

hypercar whose debt to its Sixties forebear is so strong they didn't bother to change the name. "[This car] has been designed to enhance our identity, elevate our aspirations, and embody our DNA and values," says Alfa Romeo's larger-than-life and unexpectedly sweary CEO, Jean-Philippe Imparato. "It is the brand's first custom-built car since 1969, and I promise it will not be our last. It brings Alfa Romeo back into the 'Supercar Club', of which we were one of the founding members. This car is conveying a transformation that is supporting the move of Alfa Romeo in a world that is changing."

Let's park Alfa's long-held desire to be Italy's BMW and take this thing at face value, shall we? The new car, somewhat intriguingly, can be had with either a 3.0-litre, twin turbo V6, making around 612bhp, or as a BEV that will most likely run three electric motors for more than 750bhp (it's currently under development and details remain sketchy, but only the Milano/Junior has beaten it as the company's first EV). The 33 uses a carbon fibre monocoque with aluminium front and rear subframes. And it will be manufactured in a limited run of just 33 cars by celebrated Milanese carrozzeria, Touring Superleggera.

The new 33 Stradale signals some important evolutionary steps for the company. It's the creation of Bottega, a skunkworks that Alfa Romeo says was inspired by Renaissance workshops and Sixties coachbuilders. A bespoke department, in other words, based in a room in the museum overseen by a specially convened taste *polizia*. Potential customers were invited to a secret preview in Monza during the 2022

Alfa Romeo's "Bottega" skunkworks revives the idea of a traditional Italian coachbuilder

Italian GP, where a price tag adjacent to £1.7m didn't deter eager suitors. All 33 were sold within a fortnight. We now know that the Bottega is currently working on other *fuoriserie* Alfa Romeos. From a small electric SUV to this thing is quite some bandwidth, but the Alfa brand elastic can cope with the stretch. Alejandro Mesonero-Romanos, the company's design boss, gives little away but says he's a fan of the exquisitely elfin TZ1. The Montreal is another candidate for an imaginative update. Watch this space…

The 33 Stradale isn't just a high-end brand building exercise, though, it also offers clues to the company's design trajectory. "The project has come about as a result of the passion and dedication of a small team of designers and engineers at the Alfa Romeo Centro Stile," Mesonero-Romanos asserts. "The design is inspired by Franco Scaglione's masterpiece of 1967, with a bold look to the lines of future models. A true manifesto of essential beauty."

We shall see. Channelling the spirit of a car as beloved as the original 33 Stradale is not a quest for the faint-hearted. Look at the way the late, great Marcello Gandini publicly and rather petulantly dissed 2022's limited run Lamborghini Countach LPI 800-4 when it appeared. Which raises the question, surely Alfa Romeo should be forging ahead with a vivid new design language rather than rifling through its back catalogue?

Perhaps, but in the flesh this thing is unarguable. The front end's integrated nose and wing *cofango* is pleasingly short, with a strong V-shaped section adding tension to the softer elements. The Alfa *scudetto* – shield – is here but remixed and remastered. Clients can order it in carbon fibre in classic form or in a 3D iteration. LEDs add a new graphic pulse to headlights whose shape is close to the original's expressive "eyes". Then there are the large top-hinged butterfly doors and wraparound glass, one of the stand-out features on the original. The roof is made of carbon fibre and aluminium. There's another V-section at the rear, drawing the eye to a point above the centre of a carbon fibre diffuser. More dramatic still are the rear lights, whose cylindrical form cuts deep into the rear wing.

Safe to say that fiscal pragmatism means the new 33 Stradale is not wholly new. During the big reveal in Arese, Alfa's execs delivered an impressive word salad in their efforts to distance the car from the closely related Maserati MC20 (a project that began life as an Alfa, remember, before becoming a Maserati and now finally… an Alfa). The engine is a bored-out evolution of the Giulia QF's twin turbo V6, now 3.0-litres in capacity and with new cylinder heads, but minus the Maserati Nettuno engine's clever efficiency-enhancing "pre-chamber" ignition set-up. An uprated version of the existing eight-speed DCT gearbox is fitted and there's an active rear axle. Top speed is a claimed 206mph, zero to 62mph taking less than three

> "THE 33 STRADALE OFFERS SOME IMPORTANT CLUES TO ALFA ROMEO'S FUTURE DESIGN DIRECTION"

030
SPECIFICATION

ENGINE
33 Stradale is powered by a reworked version of Giulia QF's 3.0-litre V6, also related to unit in Maserati MC20

BODY
Mixes carbon fibre and aluminium. Design is jaw-dropping 21st century reboot for 1967's original

SUSPENSION
Multi-link set-up with active dampers. Strada mode is for road use, Pista tightens everything up

AERO
V-section rear looks great but also emphasises the substantial rear diffuser. It's not a track car but it works

VEHICLE TYPE –
Mid-engined, rear-wheel drive coupe

POWERTRAIN –
3.0-litre 90-deg twin turbo V6, 612bhp @ 7,500rpm, 538lb ft @ 3,000-5,500rpm

WEIGHT: 1,500kg (dry)

DIMENSIONS –
Length: 4,637mm
Width: 1,968mm
Height: 1,226mm

TRANSMISSION –
Eight-speed dual clutch

PERFORMANCE –
Top speed 207mph (limited)
0-62mph 2.9 seconds

031
BRAIN-FRAZZLING FACT:

ALTHOUGH ONLY 18 EXAMPLES OF THE ORIGINAL ALFA ROMEO 33 STRADALE WERE PRODUCED, A HANDFUL OF CHASSIS WERE RE-PURPOSED AS CONCEPT CARS BY BERTONE, ITALDESIGN AND PININFARINA. THESE WERE THE CARABO, P33 ROADSTER, IGUANA, 33/2 COUPE SPECIALE, P33 CUNEO AND NAVAJO. THEY CAN BE SEEN ON DISPLAY IN THE ALFA ROMEO MUSEUM IN ARESE, NEAR MILAN.

seconds. A Strada mode is for less frenetic everyday driving, with a more compliant ride from the multi-link suspension and active dampers, and exhaust valve actuation only above 5,000rpm. Pista tightens everything up in all the expected parameters, but also adds a FastStart function via a Quadrifoglio button on the centre console. Braking is by Brembo, with carbon-ceramic discs. F1 driver Valterri Bottas is part of the development team. The combustion 33 weighs 1,500kg; the EV will naturally be heavier. We'll be curious to know what the ICE/EV sales mix is.

Inside, less is definitely more, perhaps even definitively. In fact, it might even be cooler than the exterior. The emphasis here is on tactility rather than technology, and Imparato insists that the 33's buyers simply didn't want lane assist and all its associated nonsense. The only voice activation is between driver and passenger. The wheel is a gorgeous three-spoke item utterly devoid of switchgear. The dashboard itself sweeps across the cabin with an intersection ahead of the passenger, while the air vents are hidden. There's a simple "3D telescopic" instrument panel – it's a fancy way of describing the old-school cowls – and a small retractable multi-media screen. Mechanical switches on the centre console governing start, drive modes and transmission are pre-eminent. There's another panel on the roof, deepening the aviation aspiration. Those amazing doors and the amount of glass used delivers a genuine cockpit feel. The rear window is made of polycarbonate.

Two different basic interior treatments are available. Tributo uses leather and aluminium with two-tone biscuit leather and slate, which is also used in the seats, dashboard, door panels and central tunnel. Alfa Corse is the more overtly sporting option, with a lots of carbon fibre and Alcantara. Red, blue or a white and red treatment that references the classic Tipo 33 race livery are the main colour options. Owners can also play around with the carbon fibre elements, and the Alfa Romeo signature on the rear is available in black, gold or silver. But if Alfa is true to its Bottega mission statement, anything is possible. This is a car that deserves the personal treatment.

Yes, we remember the Noughties 8C Competizione whose jaw-dropping looks failed to translate into a great drive. And the ill-conceived 4C is best forgotten. Defeat can still be rescued from the jaws of victory. And yes, the "new" 33 Stradale is another Alfa Romeo that's shamelessly in thrall to the company's history. But there's poetry here, too. The old boss would have lowered his fabulous eyewear, peered awhile at the car, and then smiled.

"THOSE AMAZING DOORS AND THE AMOUNT OF GLASS USED IN THE ROOF DELIVERS A GENUINE COCKPIT FEEL"

#2

WHY IT'S HERE
Because 'they' said it couldn't be done – and it almost wasn't. It's as advanced a car as has ever been attempted, and as complicated

ASTON MARTIN VALKYRIE

If you think hypercars are about maximum theatre, then the Aston Martin Valkyrie is the one for you. Getting into it is challenging enough, but that's nothing compared to the starting procedure...

Originally a collaboration between Red Bull Racing and Aston Martin, the low drag, high downforce Valkyrie concept was the brainchild of famed F1 designer Adrian Newey. That relationship dissolved when Aston formed its own F1 team, but the basics were already there: a tiny teardrop carbon fibre passenger cell with an all-new 6.5-litre naturally aspirated 65-degree V12 hard mounted to it and out back a clever gearbox integrating an electric motor. That draws power from a 1.7kWh battery pack supplied by Rimac. The powertrain is a stressed member, saving weight and allowing Aston Martin to claim a 1:1 power-to-weight ratio.

That's slipped. The V12 and e-motor still deliver a combined 1,139bhp, but weight has risen in the face of regulation, legislation and rumoured cost-cutting. As it sits here now, with brimmed tanks, it's probably around 1,350kg, which is more than we would have liked. But still, one thousand, one hundred and fifty five horsepower. Just let that sink in for a moment.

The Valkyrie is ours for the whole day, to drive around Bahrain. It's not the first place we'd have chosen for an excursion, but people's responses to a car like this are the same the world over and summed up in three letters: WTF? Our mantra as we absorb the bodywork, the gaping openings and empty spaces that define the bodywork is HITRL – how is this road legal?

But it's got numberplates and if you remove the front one, you'll find the first aid kit. Have a shunt and it will be ready distributed for your needs. A fingertip-size button releases the lightweight door. It flits up and once

The Valkyrie's cockpit is so minimal you suspect its designers would have preferred to have done away with it altogether. Below, each seat is angled inwards at two degrees and weighs just 8kg. No cupholders here

More than just a car, the Valkyrie is a collection of extraordinary design details. Tail-lights jostle for attention with a huge diffuser

you've wriggled over and down, you reach up and realise it slams with a lovely 'krump' noise. It also has soft close. Hell, it's tight in here, though. Racecar tight. You don't notice at first, but each minimalist carbon wafer seat is angled inwards at two degrees, and weighs just 8kg. That's an astonishing feat of engineering.

The upwards leg incline feels natural almost immediately. The steering wheel doesn't lift high enough, though, and an array of screens is entirely responsible for providing your rear view. A central divider prevents the passenger operating the pedals, and further back contains the parking brake switch, hazards and a USB port. But there's nowhere, not even a pouch, to put your phone. So all you can do is drop that into the slot where the crotch harness emerges from on the passenger seat. Want more storage? You'll simply have to ditch the warning triangle and inflation kit that sit under the nose. Or have a support car.

There's real complexity here. The engine takes a fair few seconds to fire, the e-motor spinning the V12 before it catches, settling into an even but raucous and penetrating idle. There are vibrations aplenty. Refinement is absent. But it operates easily. The seven-speed gearbox is a single clutch sequential by Ricardo – getting this much power and 681lb ft of torque rolling would stress the clutch hugely. So it pulls away electrically, then after that bleeds the clutch in automatically around 10mph. That never misses a beat, and happily tolerates sticky traffic all day. An amazing feat, really.

Next surprise comes as we leave the circuit. Speed bumps. The Valkyrie has a nose lift and clearance, but the suspension feels loose, soft as it drops over them. The whole aero and suspension package is designed to work together, hydraulically linked and actuated to support the car at 10mph as well as 200mph with a tonne or more of downforce on it. The sense of connection is diminished because it's not behaving as expected, the usual spring/damper activation is a nudge off normal, but this much is apparent: the ride really isn't harsh.

We're out among the oil fields now, getting more speed and flow into the Valkyrie. The low speed ride hits hard, but it smooths as speeds rise. It's a small car on the road, and forward visibility is good across the humps above the front wheels, but it's difficult to focus on individual aspects of the Valkyrie when volume dominates everything. That mighty Cosworth engine may be well-mannered and approachable, but inside it's deafening. The standard ear protection does a good filtering job, but you can't escape the mechanical thrash. We have radios to communicate but unless it's pressed to your head it may as well be a styrofoam cup.

Back on the road we start getting more of a feel for this alien machine. The gearchanges are slow and considered, the steering has weight and accuracy but not a terrific amount of natural feel. Much like most racecars. To be honest, though, the Valk's dynamic development doesn't feel quite finished.

We head to the coast, surrounded by waving arms and toots. Time to cut the shackles and blast it. Holy hell. The beast awakens, the noise instantly changes pitch and tone and the Valkyrie *shrieks*. The sound is Jurassic. Or Nineties Le Mans. You choose. Weightless acceleration, and absolutely no need to deploy the ERS button for a 140bhp e-boost. We only see 8,500rpm. Only.

The full experience on circuit the next day is mind-altering. Not just the noise, but the downforce and lack of drag means that high-speed acceleration is utterly relentless. It accelerates like a paper dart with afterburners. Here's the ultimate contrast though – we drive the Valkyrie onto a beach. It's sunset, and sadly it's not the rosy orb we were hoping for, but still offers a chance to soak in this glorious-looking thing. What a piece of sculpture, how skilfully the yin and yang of design and engineering have been blended here. The body's top surface is a distinctive flip point; underneath is insect, above is beauty.

Manama's neon does nothing to diminish this. Street lamps reflect in the front wings, each beam peeling over the curve like a shooting star. Not knowing where we're going, our local fixer jumps in the car with us. He's wearing a puffer jacket because for him 20°C ambient is freezing. It's like sharing the car with expanding foam. It's suffocating, and means you have to fight for space to operate the thing.

Could you road-trip an Aston Martin Valkyrie? Max Verstappen seems to use his on the hills and roads above Monaco pretty regularly. Yes, it has air con and that works well. And if you travel solo, you'll have space for kit. Have a dabble in the menus and you'll find the stereo controls. That's a laughable conceit. Aston did consider fitting a full-on audio system, but

"THE VALKYRIE HAS A NOSE LIFT AND SURPRISING CLEARANCE, SO SPEED BUMPS CAN BE DEALT WITH"

Above, an odd-shaped steering wheel means that big sideways action is tricky. Push a button to spin the e-motor that starts the car, before the 6.5-litre V12 erupts into action. Valkyrie uses aerospace know-how and materials

backtracked. Instead you can stream tunes through the headset, while imagining you're a WRC driver on a road section. But even so it's difficult to imagine owners tolerating this noise and sensory bombardment for long periods. Not without a support car. It's draining. We haven't been anywhere near the limits of it all day, and yet it's taken real mental processing to operate. It's not just the volume – it's the value, the foreign land, the attention, the suspension that does you in. Not entirely down to the car, then. And not repeated during next day's adrenaline fest. The Aston Martin Valkyrie overwhelms, and often feels abstract and unreal.

We stop right in the centre of the city. A nightlife hub on a weekend evening. The place throbs. It's the kind of place you might just spot one in the wild. Daft as it sounds, the Valkyrie stops people in their tracks in a way the massed ranks of McLarens and Lamborghinis lining the streets just don't. This is what happens when pedigree and exoticism are combined in this way. Aston Martin has done it, got an F1 designer's fever dream into production, breathed life into it. But at some cost.

VALKYRIE ON TRACK

There's a risk of trotting out the hypercar tester's handbook of excuses for the Aston Martin Valkyrie. It is monstrously late, hasn't ended up being entirely faithful to the original offering, and under most circumstances it's more than likely a base Porsche 911 would allow its driver to travel faster. But the handbook insists that we ignore this rather fundamental fact. As we do for most hypercars because they are the chocolate fireguards of our world and this is reason enough to love them. And doesn't it look fantastic? A futuristic amalgam of sci-fi angles and negative spaces, you walk around it wondering what bizarreness you'll see next. In some respects it

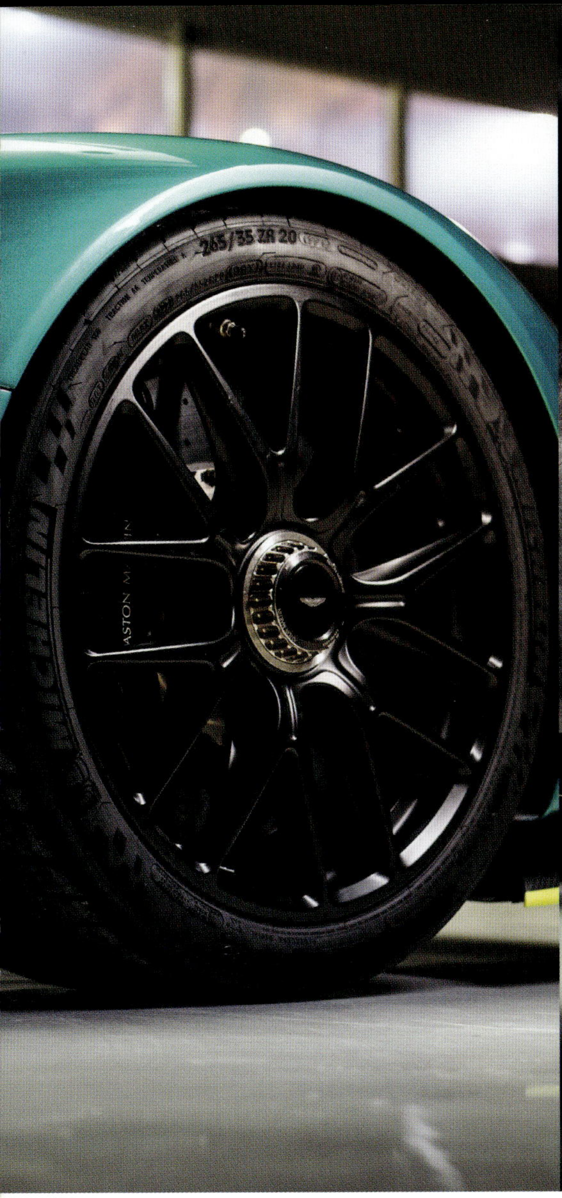
265/35 ZR 20
MICHELIN

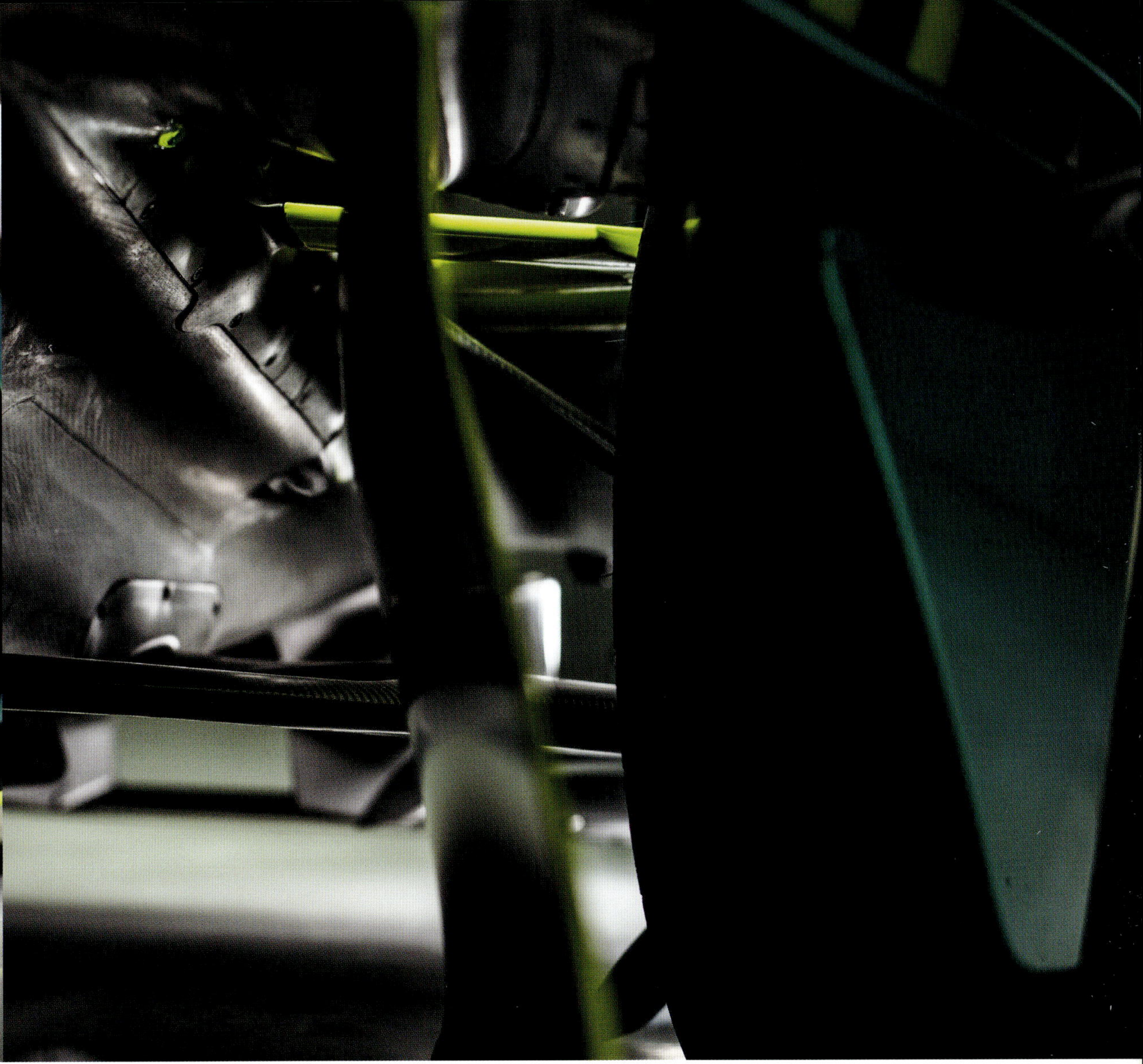

F1 AML

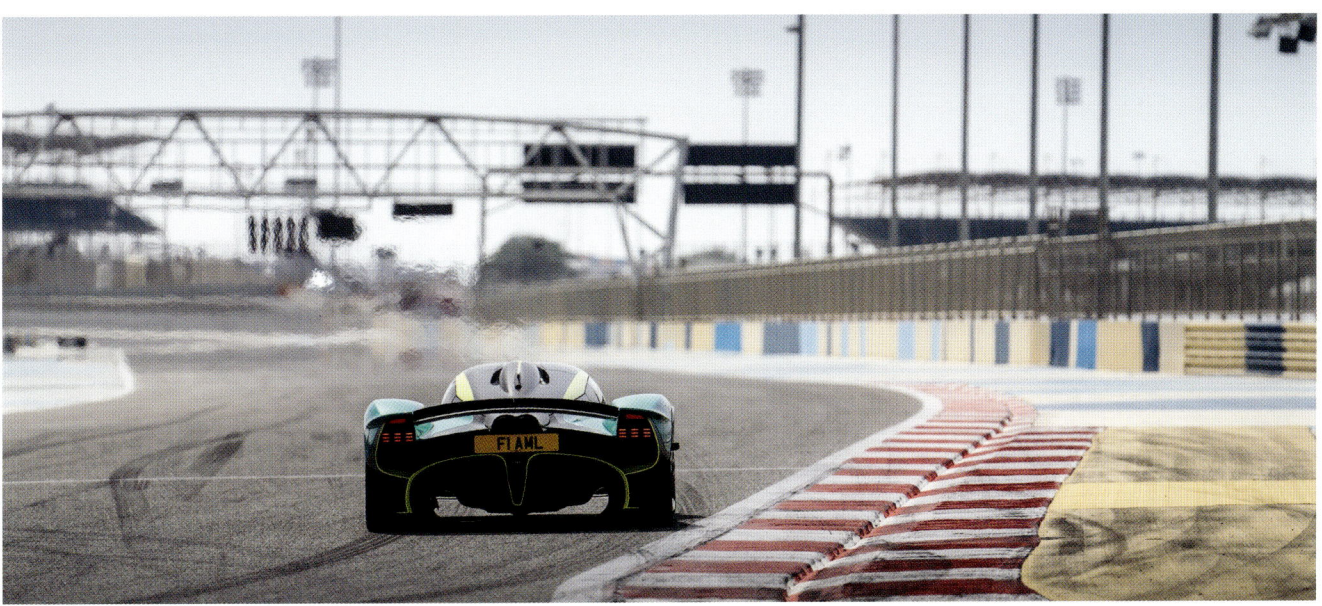

046
SPECIFICATION

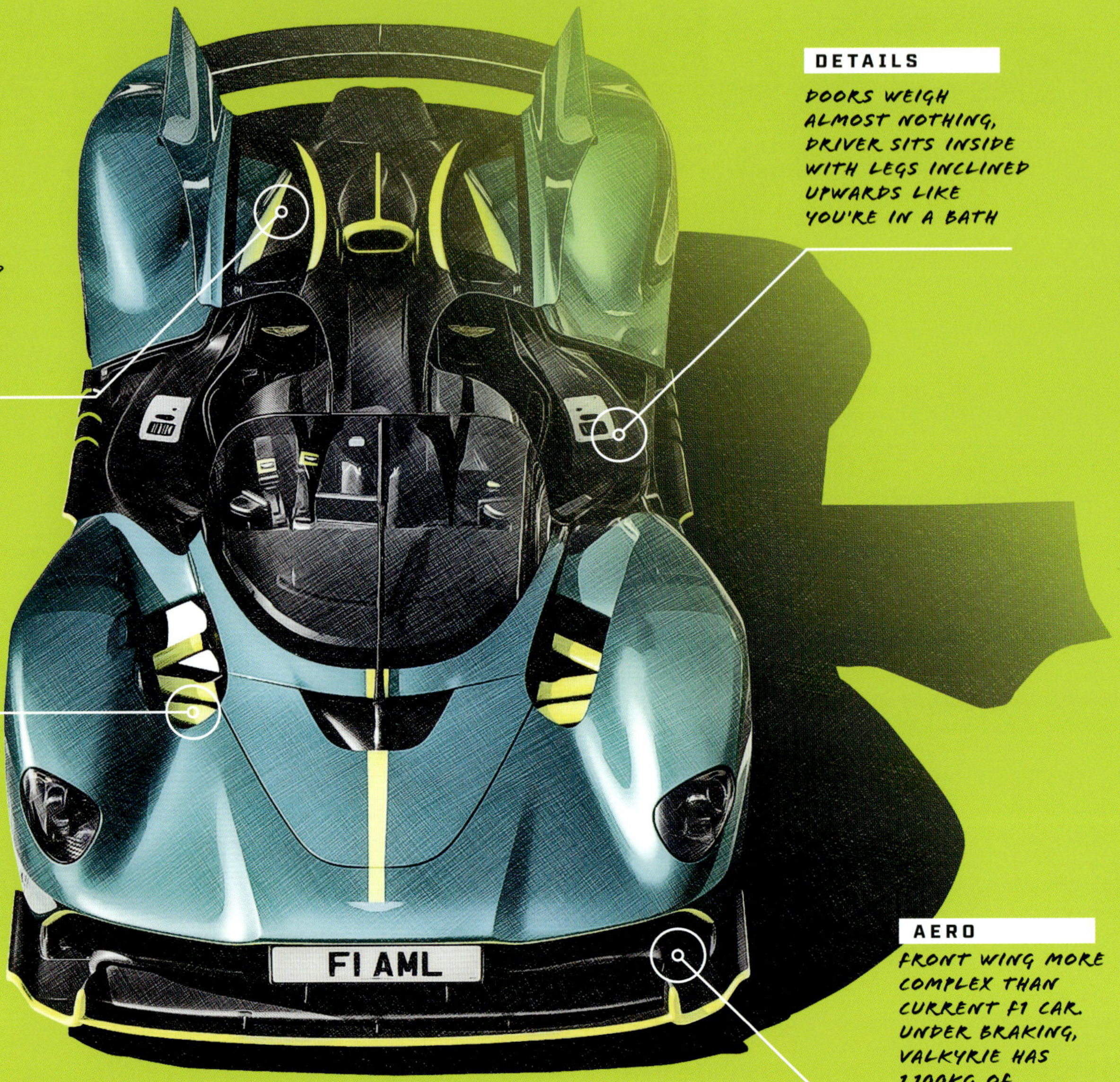

ENGINE
VALKYRIE IS POWERED BY COSWORTH-SUPPLIED 6.5-LITRE V12, MATED TO A 1.68KWH BATTERY TO PRODUCE A COMBINED 1,139BHP

DETAILS
DOORS WEIGH ALMOST NOTHING, DRIVER SITS INSIDE WITH LEGS INCLINED UPWARDS LIKE YOU'RE IN A BATH

SUSPENSION
ACTIVE SUSPENSION WORKS IN TANDEM WITH THE AERO; IT'S HYDRAULICALLY INTER-LINKED AND ACTUATED

AERO
FRONT WING MORE COMPLEX THAN CURRENT F1 CAR. UNDER BRAKING, VALKYRIE HAS 1,100KG OF DOWNFORCE

VEHICLE TYPE –
MID-ENGINED, REAR-WHEEL DRIVE COUPE

POWERTRAIN –
DOHC 48 VALVE 6.5-LITRE V12, 1,001BHP, 575LB FT – PLUS 105KW ELECTRIC MOTOR. COMBINED POWER OUTPUT 1,139BHP @ 10,600RPM, 681LB FT @ 7,000RPM; 1.7KWH LITHIUM ION BATTERY PACK

WEIGHT: 1,270KG (DRY)

DIMENSIONS –
LENGTH: 4,506MM
WIDTH: 1,920MM
HEIGHT: 1,059MM

TRANSMISSION –
SEVEN-SPEED SINGLE CLUTCH SEQUENTIAL

PERFORMANCE –
TOP SPEED 220MPH (LIMITED)
0-62MPH 2.3 SECONDS

BRAIN-FRAZZLING FACT(S):

THERE ARE SO MANY ON THIS CAR IT'S DIFFICULT TO KNOW WHICH TO INCLUDE. HOW ABOUT THE 1100KG OF DOWNFORCE IT CAN GENERATE BETWEEN 137 AND 220MPH? OR THE FACT THAT THE SHAPE OF THE WINDSCREEN MEANS THAT THE WIPER USES A TORSION BAR SO IT CAN TWIST AROUND THE SCREEN AND IS SUPPLIED BY THE SAME COMPANY THAT MADE THE WIPERS FOR THE SPACE SHUTTLE?

could be argued that cars like this are better left as static objects, best demonstrated by others so we can all hear them and see them scream past. On the other hand, we have a circuit to ourselves.

The Valkyrie is initially very intimidating on a circuit, a situation not helped if you have had time behind the wheel of the AMR Pro. From the start the road car feels quite compromised and much heavier. The seating position is amusing for the first few minutes, and the contact surfaces are lovingly trimmed, which is a nice touch. There's an air of fighter pilot or *Star Wars* speeder about the Valkyrie as you slide down low and under the wheel. The view forwards is just about enough, the rest is typically woeful. A rear camera does help ever so slightly.

We venture out on a set of new Michelin Cup 2 tyres to get a feel for over 1,100bhp. Even when cold, the engine's vibrations trace a different path through the carbon tub and into your body. The noise inside is certainly impressive, but it's mostly volume over quality. Like the Porsche Carrera GT, folk on the outside get a better deal.

Not much happens below 3,500rpm, then the V12 begins to push hard, the gnashing increases and at that point – as the afterburners hit – it becomes very difficult to see the wheel mounted speedometer. How or why a clean sheet car of this type has a steering wheel that won't adjust high enough for most drivers is a mystery.

What happens next might compensate for that ergonomic faux pas. Because the Valkyrie piles on some big, big numbers – it's ferociously fast and you have to keep looking down to ensure you don't hit the 11,100rpm limiter. Into the first braking zone the left pedal is very long, but the feel is good and the graunching of ABS gubbins is reassuring when you're casually hitting 210mph on the main straight. But the gearshifts need discussing because they are just so slow on the way up. This frantic V12 masterpiece rushes to potential valve bounce and just when you want a whip-crack shift, the clutch disengages and slurs a shift that is so slow it actually interrupts your appreciation of the engine. Presumably this is in order to protect something in the powertrain, but it kills some of the car's potential theatre.

The handling on track is quite difficult to decipher. We're in Bahrain, which is always dusty off line, and the car mostly wants to understeer. But there's a complete lack of traction and the damping is just odd – it feels like the clever hydraulic suspension is struggling to glean anything through the Cup 2's sidewalls and just throws support at whichever corner it fancies. Something isn't right. A change to Cup 2Rs makes a huge difference. Now you can push much deeper into braking zones and hold the racing line, but the steering is heavy and the car is physical to drive fast. And it's just so, *so* loud. Above 50mph there's no point in trying to talk to whoever is wedged in beside you. Every journey requires the use of in-built ear defenders.

If the gearbox limits the engine, then the tyre limits the Valkyrie's chassis. The vastly complicated hydraulic system that is allegedly a large part of the reason why the car was delayed is also difficult to fathom. It's designed to offer a range of ride height and damping options that conventional suspension simply can't replicate. On track it doesn't give a great sense of connection and the car feels quite inert mid-corner because with the systems on, the throttle is killed too early. This isn't a car to play with in a turn, partly because the steering wheel is such an odd shape. In fact, it may not be possible to correct a large slide. If only Aston could have developed a tyre especially for this car, maybe the chassis could have been more playful.

So where does that leave us? Dynamically, we expected more. The Aston Martin Valkyrie is potentially the greatest hypercar ever made, but it just isn't finished. The electronic chassis systems are poorly calibrated, the gearbox is just too slow and the noise makes it unlikely that people will ever want to use it as a motor car. Those are all attributes of a mid-to-late stage development vehicle. If I was a customer, I'd find that deeply disappointing, regardless of the immense challenge this car represents.

However, there is much to be said in the Aston Martin Valkyrie's defence. It didn't miss a beat in nearly two days of stop-start driving in a warm climate. The same couldn't be said of the Mercedes AMG One. The aesthetic package combined with the V12 are enough to elevate this car beyond anything else that has ever been sold before, and let's face it, that's how most owners will use their £2.5m investment. And the history of this type of machine is littered with compromised glory. In fact, arguably the daddy of them all – the McLaren F1 – was a a sensational engine in a chassis that probably needed some more development work. That the Valkyrie appears to have replicated exactly the same outcome almost 30 years later could be seen as a triumph or a failure. That is one for us all to ponder.

Ultimately, we're really glad it exists because there's a strong suspicion that it very nearly didn't. The Valkyrie is an epic machine in so many ways. But it's frustrating to know that there's a truly history-changing vehicle just waiting to be unlocked from underneath that extraordinary bodywork.

"THE STEERING IS HEAVY AND IT'S A PHYSICAL CAR TO DRIVE FAST. THE V12 ENGINE IS A MASTERPIECE"

Top, that is a Valkyrie being cornered very hard indeed. It's just difficult to tell, such is its immense body control. Left, somehow Aston Martin's engineers managed to fit a 6.5-litre V12 engine

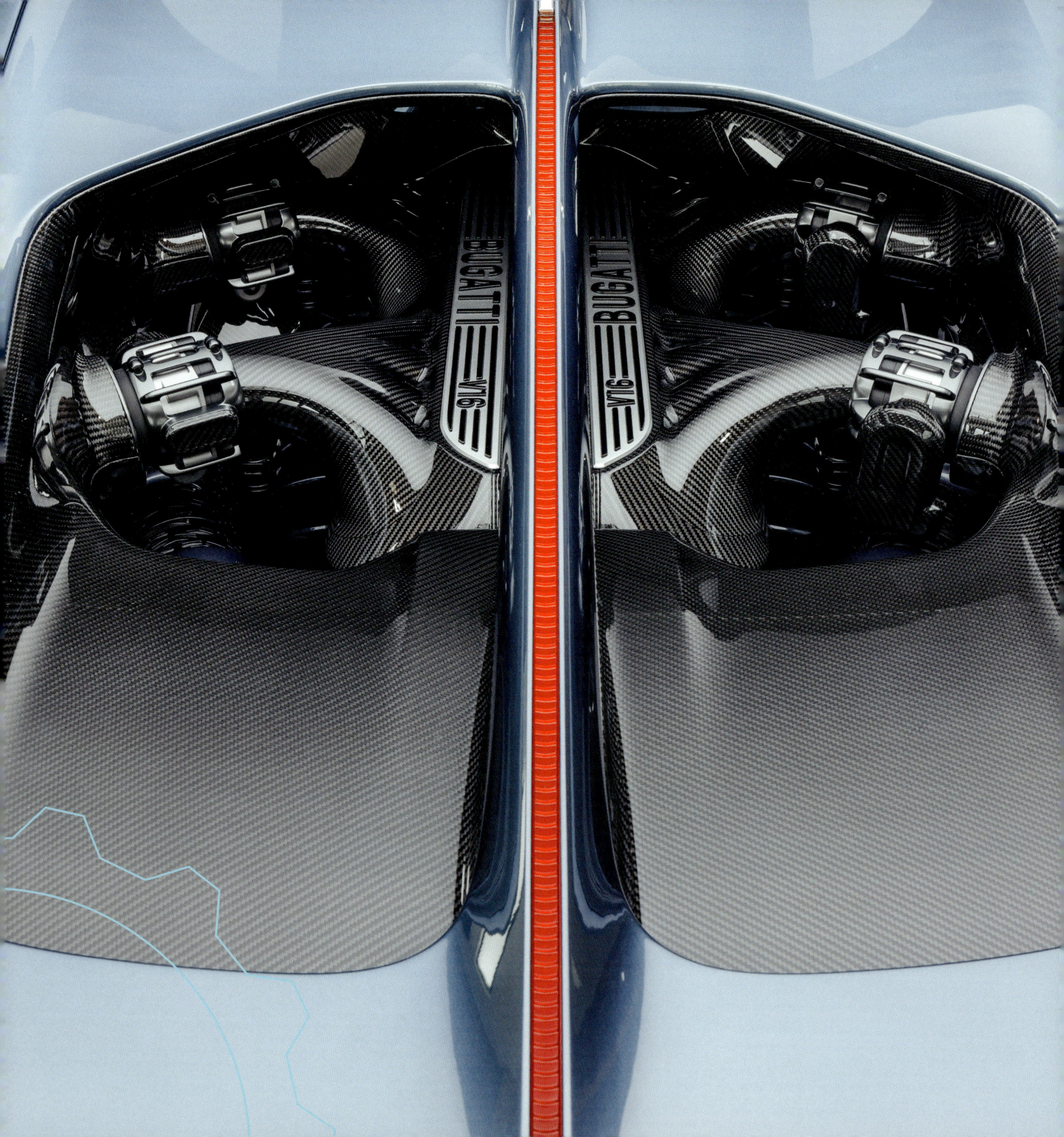

 # 3

WHY IT'S HERE
Powered by an astonishing new 8.3-litre V16 engine and three electric motors, Bugatti is thinking long term on the Tourbillon

BUGATTI TOURBILLON

Mate Rimac, the annoyingly young and freakishly switched-on CEO of Bugatti-Rimac, could have given himself a few years to get his feet under the table. After all, he'd already spent half a decade developing the 1,888bhp, pure-electric Rimac Nevera, the world's fastest road car. Surely a Bugatti-shaped re-body and a herd of new leather on the inside would do the trick and drag the company into the EV age? Not comfortable with ditching combustion completely? Fair enough, a hybridised version of the Chiron's quad-turbo W16 engine could easily tickle the heights of 2,000bhp. Needless to say, that's not how he saw things panning out.

"Sure, the Nevera could be a Bugatti if you re-skin it. Financially it's the obvious choice, but it's absolutely the wrong decision, which is why I fought against it so hard. Bugatti is all about heritage, craftsmanship, quality and performance, but it's more aristocratic, it's about staying in the analogue world," says Rimac, who is giving us the grand tour. "Then I thought, 'OK, let's take the Chiron and make it hybrid.' But that's also bad because it would be super heavy, everything would be compromised. So I came up with a crazy proposal to make a completely new car." A sentence guaranteed to bring the bean counters out in hives, but the rest of us in rapturous applause because, yes, a 36-year-old holds Bugatti's future in his hands. His is a fighter's spirit and he appears to know exactly what his clients want.

Four years of boardroom scuffles later and the result is this, the 1,775bhp Bugatti Tourbillon. It's named after a (usually exposed) mechanism in silly-money

Above, as the name suggests, the design ethos of the Bugatti Tourbillon was inspired by the ultra-precise engineering of haute horologie. The instrument cluster uses sapphires and rubies in its construction. Below, CEO Mate Rimac is an EV pioneer but he knows that Bugatti has to retain some old-school elements to survive

Left, seats in the Tourbillon are fixed to the floor for lightness and positioning. The audio system uses actuators in the door panels rather than traditional speakers. Below, the only screen in the car remains hidden unless the driver wants to see it

Left, the Tourbillon develops Bugatti design language in evolutionary yet spectacular fashion. The iconic horse-shoe line is a key graphic

watches that counters the negative effects of gravity to improve accuracy. It's a nod to Rimac's obsession with beautiful, exposed mechanical engineering, and possibly the new Bugatti's commitment to picking a fight with physics. It's a car that's 33mm lower and no longer than a Chiron, despite harbouring an all-new 9,000rpm 8.3-litre V16 engine with a metre-long crankshaft and an eight-speed dual-clutch gearbox bolted to the back. It weighs fractionally less than the Chiron's 1,995kg, despite packing a 200kg, 25kWh battery down the spine where the gearbox would normally be, two electric motors on the front axle, another on the rear – and takes advantage of that slimmer centre console to pinch the glasshouse and reduce frontal area and therefore drag. Lighter, more powerful and more slippery than a car capable of well over 300mph… the Tourbillon (impossible to say minus a French accent, like 'croissant') is not cocking about.

By now, you may well have remarked that the Tourbillon looks somewhat familiar, and we don't disagree. But take a beat, and observe the floating headlights hanging on flying buttresses designed to feed as many precious air molecules as possible into the ravenous naturally aspirated engine. Notice how the narrower glasshouse accentuates the shoulders and that the doors are pure theatre – dihedral and electrically operated, a double Bugatti first. At the rear, things really kick off – an exposed V16, visibly tipped forward to accommodate the upward slope of the enormous venturi tunnels that run either side. A diffuser with twice the volume of the Chiron's means the deployable spoiler can stay tucked away on Vmax runs, but pops up as an air-brake and in Track mode. Then there are the 3D-printed titanium exhaust tips sitting up high, while from behind the rear tyres are fully exposed like some huge, uber-luxe hot-rod. Follow a Tourbillon and stone chips may occur.

"It would be easy to say, 'OK, let's make a statement that it's a new company, it's new management, it's a new powertrain, so let's really make something wacky.' And actually we had some proposals like that, but it felt wrong. We think long term. This is a brand that's existed for 114 years and we wanted to exist for another 100-plus," Mate explains in his customary enthusiastic manner. "It's so precious to have these Bugatti design elements that you recognise from afar – the horseshoe, the centre line, the two-tone paint. It would be such a shame to throw it away."

Performance is largely theoretical at this stage (first deliveries aren't until 2026, so real-world testing has only just begun in earnest) but reliably incomprehensible. We're promised a total of 1,800bhp: 1,000bhp from the engine, 800bhp from the e-motors, meaning that without even waking the V16 from its slumber you have all-wheel drive, a 37-mile EV-only range, Ferrari 812 Superfast levels of grunt… and happy neighbours. Mate is keen to point out that when you're in EV mode, you won't wake the engine even when you floor it, not until you're out of charge at least. Equally, when you want the engine on for the full operatic fanfare, it stays on.

Top speed is limited to 277mph, which should keep you covered day-to-day, but clearly there's more to give. Will Bugatti go after a new top speed record? "Let's see," says Mate, which means "yes". Andy Wallace, the man who'll probably pilot it into uncharted territory, points out that it gets the "boring bit, up to 250mph" done so much faster than the Chiron (around 25 seconds versus 32.6) that it'll give them so much more of the 5.4-mile Ehra-Lessien straight to play with when pushing beyond 300mph. Speculation time: is 500km/h (311mph) possible? Certainly. How about 320mph? We wouldn't put it past them, or Andy's bottle for that matter.

A veritable missile then, but one with an attention-to-detail not generally seen this side of a Pagani. "Normally you have exterior design and interior design, but even when this car's naked we want it to look special, so we employed a rolling chassis designer," Mate tells us with a huge grin (CEO: one, finance department: nil). Frankly, Mate's wins are everywhere. All the hinges are anodised and machine aluminium. "I'm a bit of a hinge freak," he admits. Twinned with dual-valve active dampers, the suspension arms are 3D printed by Divergent (the sister company to Czinger, as seen elsewhere in this book) because they're stiffer, stronger and also more beautiful. Parts of this thing are organically grown like sinew and bone.

"THE TOP SPEED IS LIMITED TO 277MPH, WHICH SHOULD KEEP YOU COVERED, BUT THERE'S EVEN MORE TO COME"

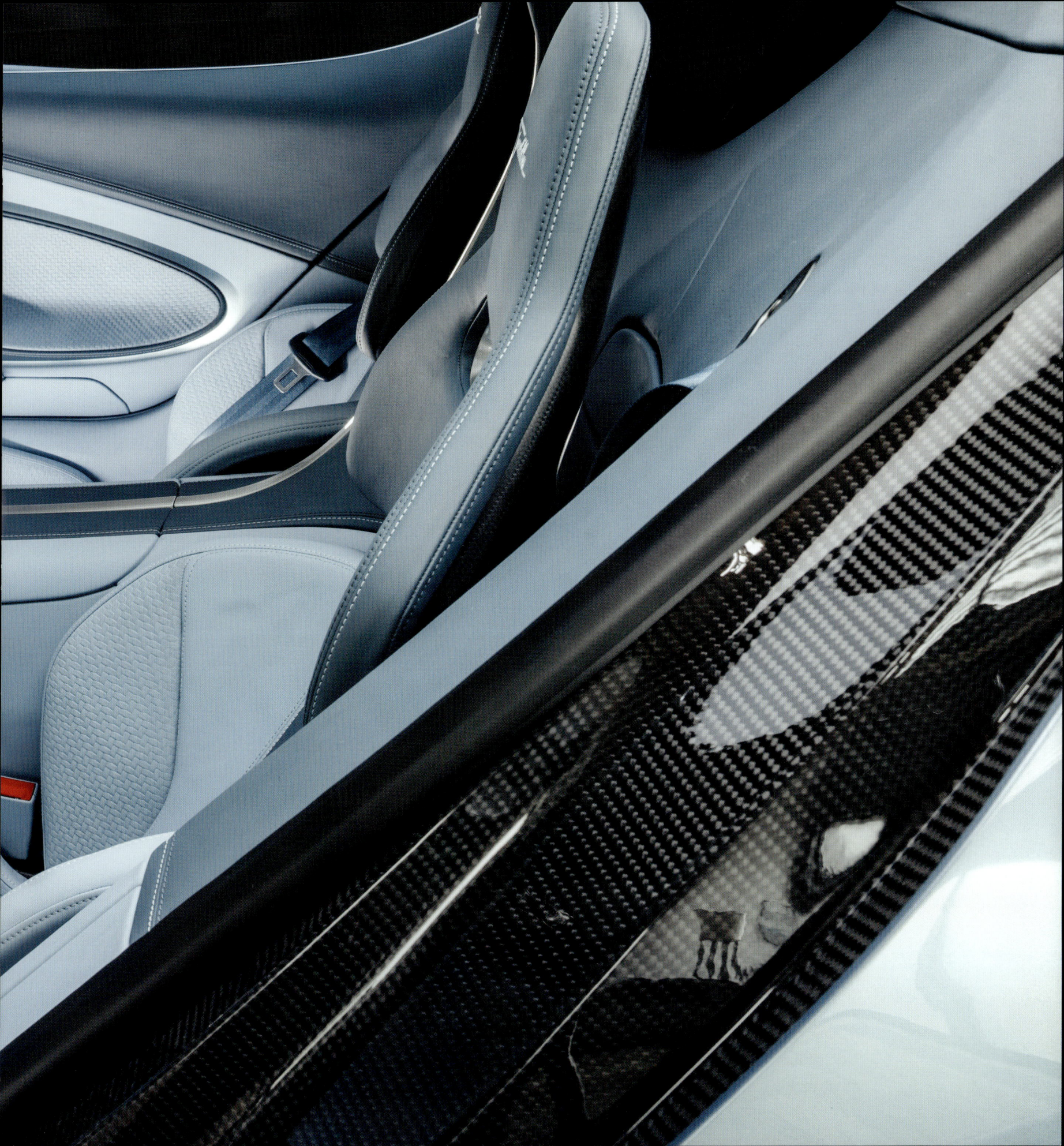

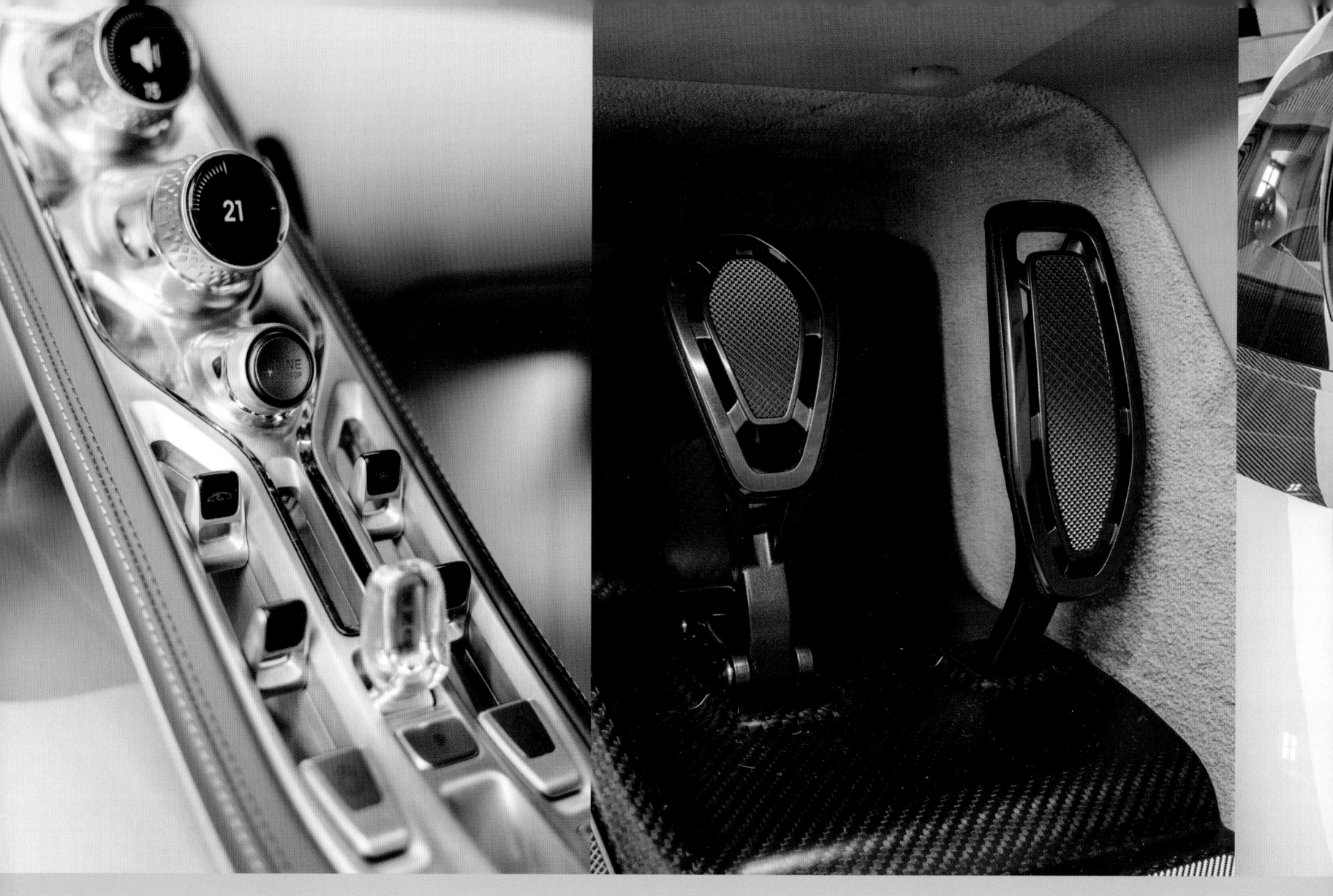

Above, Bugatti Tourbillon uses the most extreme materials to deliver maximum tactility. The driver pulls an organ stop lever on the dash to start the engine. Even the pedals are artful

And we haven't even climbed inside yet. Allow the door to open itself and take a moment to marvel at the precision of the exposed carbon tub along the sill, take a lungful of very expensive smelling leather and dive in… To find tactile mechanical wonders wherever you look. The skeletonised instrument dials are essentially Swiss chronographs scaled up, with every cog and jewel on view. Two needles on the centre dial take care of revs (the dial goes to 10,000rpm) and speed (all the way to 550km/h – that's 341mph). On the left there's analogue battery, oil temp and fuel gauges, on the right dual needles showing real-time power draw from the motors and ICE engine – simply add them together to find out how brave your right foot is. The real showstopper, though, is a two-spoke wheel that orbits the stationary centre boss and instruments, with the paddle shifters hinged from the rim. It's mesmerising, until we point out that the Citroen C4 Picasso had something similar, which rather kills the mood.

A strip of dials on the machined crystal glass centre console, plus the seat adjustment knob on the door, also have exposed internal organs, and there's a delightfully tactile way of firing up the engine – by pulling an organ stop lever that protrudes from the dash. The seats are fixed longitudinally (an important move to keep the car's overall length down), but they can be raised and the back angle adjusted, after which you move the pedal box to suit. And what's this? No screens? Almost. Hit a button and a portrait-oriented display rises from the top of the dash before rotating to landscape and settling back down in an outrageously satisfying piece of mechanical ballet. A must-have for the reversing camera in some markets, but Mate also hates drivers having to follow sat-nav instruction on their phones, balanced precariously on their lap. Here you get a super-simple interface with Apple CarPlay and Android Auto connectivity.

Everywhere you look and feel, then, is a feast of handcrafted, milled or printed unobtanium.

062
SPECIFICATION

BODY & CHASSIS
TOURBILLON IS MADE OF NEXT-GEN T800 CARBON COMPOSITE, PACKAGE IS THE SAME AS CHIRON DESPITE ADDITION OF FRONT E-AXLE, DUAL E-MOTORS AND INVERTER

DOORS
DOORS ARE DIHEDRAL AND ELECTRICALLY OPERATED, ADMITTING OCCUPANTS TO AN INTERIOR INSPIRED BY THE INTRICACIES OF A SWISS WATCH

ENGINE
MOTIVE FORCE COMES FROM AN ALL-NEW 8.3-LITRE V16 NAT ASP UNIT & THREE ELECTRIC MOTORS FOR TOTAL OF 1,775BHP

AERO
DIFFUSER IS BUILT AROUND A NEW CRASH CONCEPT AND IS MOSTLY SUBMERGED WITHIN THE STRUCTURE ITSELF

VEHICLE TYPE –
MID-ENGINED, ALL-WHEEL DRIVE COUPE

POWERTRAIN –
8.3-LITRE V16, NATURALLY ASPIRATED, WITH THREE 250KW ELECTRIC MOTORS. COMBINED POWER OUTPUT IS 1,775BHP, 37-MILE RANGE ON E-POWER ALONE

WEIGHT: 1,990KG APPROX

DIMENSIONS –
LENGTH: 4,671MM
WIDTH: 2,051MM
HEIGHT 1,189MM

TRANSMISSION –
EIGHT-SPEED DUAL-SHIFT GEARBOX

PERFORMANCE –
0-62MPH 2.0 SECONDS
0-186MPH LESS THAN 10 SECONDS
TOP SPEED 277MPH

063
BRAIN-FRAZZLING FACT:

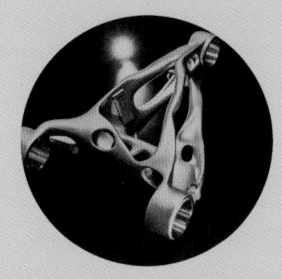

AS WELL AS AN EXTERIOR AND INTERIOR HEAD OF DESIGN, THE TOURBILLON ALSO HAD A DESIGNER DEDICATED TO ITS CHASSIS. "WE WANTED SOMEONE TO TAKE ANY PIECE OF THIS CAR, FROM INSIDE, OUTSIDE, OR UNDER THE SKIN, AND BELIEVE THAT IT COULD BE PLACED IN AN ART GALLERY," SAYS BUGATTI'S PRESIDENT, CHRISTOPHE PIOCHON. IT'S A METHODOLOGY THAT COMPANY FOUNDER ETTORE BUGATTI EMPLOYED BACK IN THE DAY. HE LAVISHED THE SAME ATTENTION ON EVERY COMPONENT – EVEN THE ONES THAT YOU COULDN'T SEE.

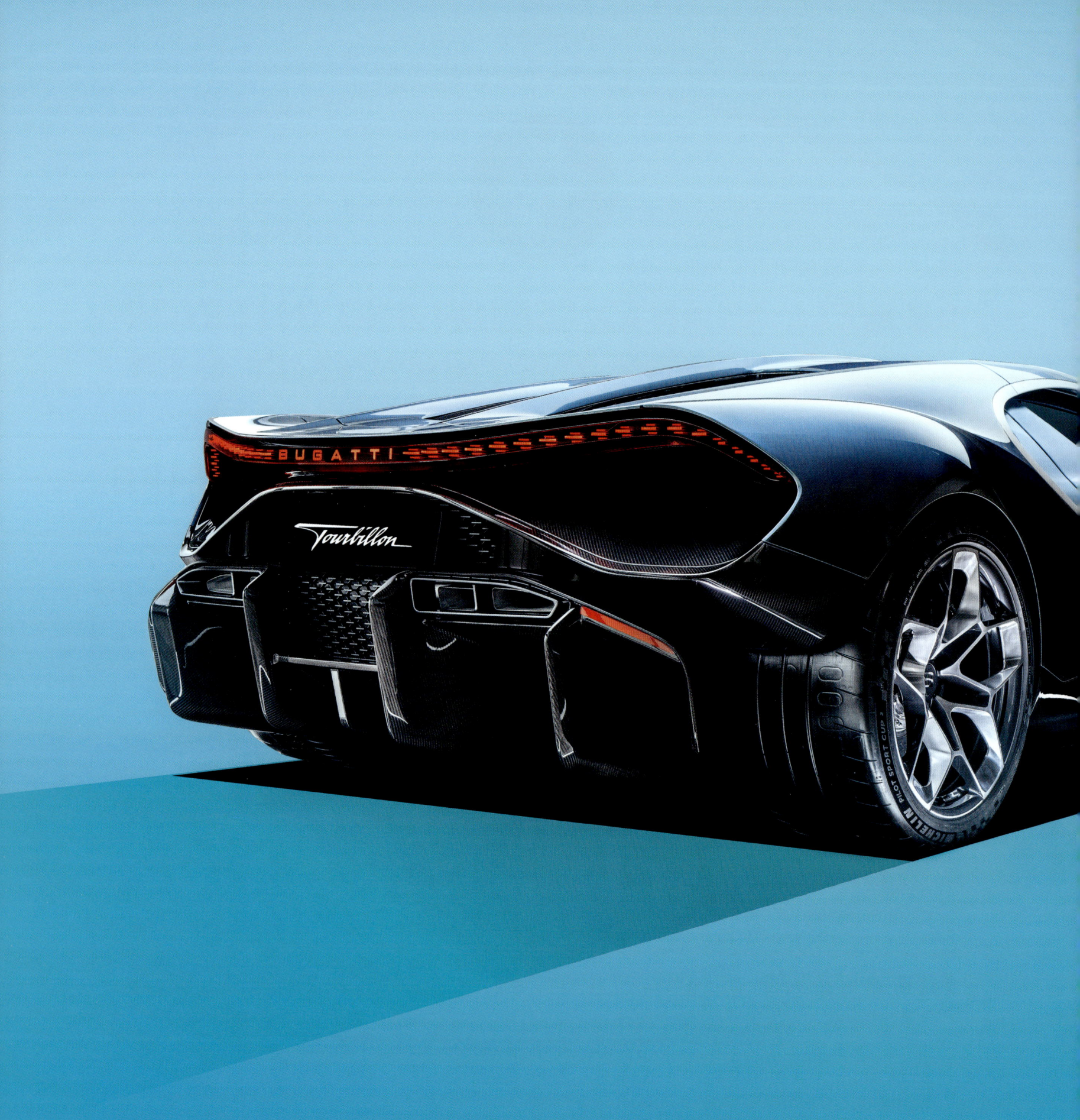

Left, Bugatti Tourbillon uses some of the most advanced aerodynamic solutions ever applied to a road car, including a number of patented technologies. The rear view is dominated by the diffuser and exposed rear tyres

Exotic materials, thoughtful touches, a sense of something approaching value for your €3.8m (£3.2m) plus tax. That's in excess of £4m with a few choice options. This is now a self-funding company, remember. Gone are the billions of VW investment that built the modern Bugatti brand, so proceeds from sales need to fund the next round of development and manufacturing. And the key to turning a profit seems to be Rimac's willingness to work with top-tier suppliers where appropriate, rather than going the full-Koenigsegg and making absolutely everything in-house. The brakes are from Brembo, Concepto supplies the instrument dials, Cosworth the engine (they're busy guys), Divergent 3D for the suspension, and of course Rimac Technology for the electronics.

"The key is we worked super closely together – the designers, the engineers and myself – from the beginning on every detail," says Mate. "Because if you come to this stage and say, 'I don't like something,' it's impossible to change. You throw the timing and money out of the window. We executed on the initial idea, and managed to get it exactly the way it was envisioned in the beginning."

And with that he strolls over to a battered cardboard box and pulls out a simple, 3D-printed plastic model of a rolling chassis. "We made this in June 2020, so four years ago. It already had the naturally aspirated V16, the gearbox behind the engine with the electric motor behind that, and two electric motors in the front. It's the model I took to the VW Group CEO Herbert Diess to explain what I wanted to do with the brand." So the Tourbillon isn't just a new performance benchmark, it's a victory for combustion and analogue mechanical complexity in a world being frog-marched towards EVs. Or as Mate puts it, "a hypercar that says yes to progress, but not at the expense of emotion."

4

WHY IT'S HERE
The most intriguing hypercars don't play by the rules. And this one changes pretty much everything

CZINGER 21C

Start with a love of superbikes, apply some of that thinking, and you've got yourself a Czinger 21C – complete with one-plus-one seating position. And a manufacturing proposition that turns traditional thinking on its head

"Here's what it is man. I want to build really bad-ass stuff, but if you're a craftsman who is actually a technologist, you need to create the right tools. I want this car company Czinger to be five blocks ahead of anybody else on the planet in creating these tools and expressing them as the cutting edge of the mind…"

Meet Kevin Czinger, founder of Czinger Vehicles. Not your average CEO. A man of humble beginnings from Cleveland, Ohio, the first to go to college from his "very working class family", where "nobody cracked open a book", who cites watching Jacob Bronowski's *The Ascent of Man* in 1973 – a BBC-produced series that plotted the history of humankind, showing how art, creativity and technology were entirely interwoven – as the point when something clicked. And here we are, half a century later, standing next to the Czinger 21C – a stretched slice of carbon fibre, wings and voids with enough firepower to skin a Chiron, and secrets cradled within it that could alter the car industry forever.

Were you to choose this moment to scoff loudly and dismiss Czinger (silent C, like the tower burger) as another prime piece of vapourware, we wouldn't blame you. The gutter of supercar history is clogged with ambitious start-ups like this, but Czinger's endgame isn't just to sell 80 (25 track, 55 road) 21Cs for $1.7m a pop. His mission is to change the way cars are designed and built through the freedom of 3D printing and a revolutionary manufacturing process designed to de-materialise and de-capitalise everything… The 21C is merely a proof of concept.

"This is a car I've dreamed of. And if you have the tools to build something that's totally off the hook, go for it." That's Kevin again. We're walking around his vision in naked carbon and you can forget classic mid-engine proportions – the 21C is a shape-shifter. Long and low from the side, a single curve sweeping from nose to tail, but then narrow as you circle around. From the front, a windscreen that originates ahead of the front axle; from the rear, a wing, diffuser and mesh, mainly.

Distinctive looks were baked in from the moment Kevin insisted on a one-plus-one layout. "I love superbikes. Being in that centre driving position

Left, the radical design is way more than skin deep. High-load areas of the Czinger chassis and structure are 3D-printed, including the wishbones in the suspension

When is a wheel not a wheel? When it's part of "an infinite expression of unique creativity"

is optimal from a driving, handling and emotional standpoint," he says. Slide your backside over the wide sill and drop into the driver's seat and it's apparent he's not wrong. Even at a stand-still there's an immediate sense of focus. In a McLaren F1 or Speedtail you're flanked by your passengers, practically wearing them as shoulder pads, but here you're on your own. Even with a passenger in the back, legs akimbo, you'll soon forget they're there. Just don't compare this to a Renault Twizy. The problem with a one-plus-one, mid-engined car is there's quite a lot of human to fit in before you get to the oily bits. Hence the driver's seat pushed right to the pointy end of the car, and an engine slung out over the rear axle. "Yes, it's a challenge, but what the heck is life for?"

Ready for the numbers? Please adopt the brace position. The engine is an in-house developed 2.9-litre twin turbo V8 producing 937bhp with an 11,000rpm red line, although it could go to 13,000 as one of the engineers — a former Koenigsegg employee — casually explains. It'll be the world's most power-dense production engine, connected to a seven-speed sequential gearbox. On the front axle are two electric motors fed by a 2kWh lithium-titanate (faster to charge and discharge than normal lithium-ion) battery pack housed in the sills and kept topped up by a rear motor generator. In the non-homologated launch car they contribute a further 237bhp for four-wheel drive and a grand total of 1,174bhp. Which is a lot. The kerbweight is 1,165kg, which isn't. "I love Bruce Lee. I'm not an Arnie Schwarzenegger guy. The future is about being lean and mean and efficient, it's all about power to weight."

"THIS ISN'T JUST A CAR. CZINGER IS A COMPANY WITH A BIG IDEA MAKING AS MUCH NOISE AS IT POSSIBLY CAN"

We agree, but this is silly. The claimed performance figures are 0–60mph in 1.9 seconds, a quarter mile in 8.3secs at 170mph and a top speed of 236mph, despite 790kg of downforce at 155mph. The more slippery, fully homologated road-biased version provides more hybrid assistance for a total of 1,233bhp, although it weighs a bit more at 1,250kg. Hardly a fatty. Top speed climbs to a tyre-troubling 268mph.

But those are just the titillating headlines. Only when you see a bare chassis do you get a sense of how different it is. Any sections, especially high-load areas, that can be 3D printed, are. Everything from the suspension wishbones to front crash structure, windscreen surround to dashboard is ctrl+P in aluminium and titanium alloys. Wherever possible, printed nodes are joined by cost-saving, off-the-shelf materials – like carbon-fibre tubes and standard-sized aluminium extrusions to create a super-stiff and beautiful structure. You see, the software that designs the printed components only puts material where it really needs to be, in the process creating mesmerising, organic shapes that flow like tendons and muscle.

So there are gains in rigidity, cost benefits in fewer raw materials and it's easily recyclable. At the end of a 3D-printed component's life you melt it, shoot nitrogen through it and it returns to a powder, ready to be printed again. Then there's the multi-purpose perks – stuff like the exhaust muffler, designed by Czinger's software to act not only as a silencer but as an integral part of the rear crash structure. Proper joined-up thinking. You'll also note a 3D-printed rectangular exhaust tip – created so it can spit X-shaped flames on the overrun.

Cool, but not the full picture. Because it's Czinger's DAPS (Divergent Adaptive Production System) that rips up the traditional car building business model. By splitting a factory into any number of 15m x 15m fully automated "cells", each capable of assembling up to 10,000 chassis a year – that's one every 20 minutes or so – and costing just $2.5m upfront for the robots and other hardware, "we've turned Henry Ford on his head," says Kevin.

You'll still need a climate-controlled 3D-printing lab churning out components on site and some extra space for final assembly by humans, but it reduces start-up costs for a new company exponentially. And because there's no tooling, flexibility is through the roof. If one model isn't selling well and another is, you simply switch that cell to produce the more popular version and meet demand. You needn't sink gazillions into a gigafactory based on vague predictions, you start small and scale up.

But still, we're scratching the surface. Kevin's ultimate vision is an "infinite expression of unique creativity". Translated into English that means powerful software into which you put your needs; a computer then performs all the engineering calculations and outputs the components you need. Just press print, assemble, and the car is yours. "We're only at a sub-systems level now," Kevin tells us, "but full vehicle integration isn't far off." Imagine an online vehicle configurator that doesn't just let you choose your trim and paint, you could lay out the exact shape, size and capabilities you need, pay less for it, and tread more lightly on the environment.

"This isn't a Lego block kit. This is a kit that says 'before you touch the first Lego block, you've customised every single block you're going to use,'"

Everything on the Czinger 21C is all-new or completely reimagined. Including the in-house developed 2.9-litre twin turbo V8, good for 937bhp. It's the world's most power dense production engine

Kevin explains patiently. "After that you want to build something else? Just push it aside and customise every Lego block again, and they're all interdependent and interrelated. That's what digital manufacturing is in the end. We're not going to be a supplier, we're going to be a licenser of those tools."

The 21C has four wheels and an engine, enough power to reverse the earth's rotation, and belongs on a teenager's bedroom wall. Is it a car? Not really. It's a company with a big idea making noise in the most engaging way possible. And that big idea is sufficiently different to get our attention.

Want an idea of how abnormally rapid the Czinger 21C is? We've just watched, hands on cheeks from the pitlane, as it ripped its own roof off down the straight at Willow Springs. A polycarbonate panel peeled back like a can of tuna and sent cartwheeling into the air… ta-da! The Czinger 21C Spider gets an early, unexpected reveal.

To be fair, it did have one of our GoPros suckered to it (with Czinger's permission), which at somewhere north of 150mph was clearly undoing the good work of that wing, and imparting some fairly serious lift. Cue a swift operation to reattach with black tack and gaffer tape. Good as new.

Apparently the beautifully finished bodywork, perched atop this prototype chassis and powertrain, was only fitted a few weeks ago to give potential customers something to coo over at Monterey Car Week. It had only been driven up to 20mph until now. Oh well, such are the trials and errors of working with an early car, and we could hardly turn down the opportunity, could we?

Rewind four hours and more fun and games. We're on the road, about 20 minutes from Willow, surrounded by a forest of wind turbines whistling gently in the breeze. We're currently sweating like a sumo wrestler playing squash, and not because there's no aircon yet but because we've stalled on the wrong side of the road while turning left. A minivan has just crested the hill and approaches at speed. Fortunately, Kevin Czinger (the boss) and Luiz Oliveira (head of powertrain) leap to our rescue from the car in front and flag the traffic down as we restart the engine, bung a load of revs at it and haul ourselves out of harm's way.

You see, the 21C currently has a straight cut racing-style dog box and a hair trigger hand

clutch for getting off the line, which makes things tricky, especially when you're turning hard left and the paddle has to swap hands as you're feeding it out. On the flat, you can employ the two e-motors on the front axle to get you rolling forwards, and use that momentum to smooth the process, but we'd stopped on an upslope, which negated the creep. Fortunately, it's a temporary solution – a new Xtrac single-clutch auto arrives soon, which promises to make low speed stuff not quite as embarrassingly life or death.

Spool back further to the previous afternoon and we're on Spunky Canyon Road – chosen for its topography, not comedic value – for perhaps the most bizarre moment of all. It's our first taste of piloting the 21C: an opportunity to drink in the brilliance of the central driving position and the 360° visibility as the scenery rushes past the windows and the clouds slide by overhead. Propulsion, however, comes not from the V8 behind, nor the motors out front, but by lifting our foot from the brake. Gravity is our fuel as we freewheel down a long hill to get some quality car-to-car photography in the bag.

Why? Because Czinger's new engine guru (former power unit engineer at Mercedes-AMG F1, a man who knows a thing or two about high-performance hybrids) Luiz Oliveira is on a plane back from his holidays in Hawaii and they don't want to fire it up without his laptop close at hand. Rewind a bit more, and our 21C odyssey started earlier that day on a high – at the Blackbird Airpark in Palmdale, California. We arrive to find the 21C not being upstaged despite being the meat in a supersonic stealth plane sandwich. On one side the SR-71 Blackbird, on the other its precursor the A-12 – still the fastest manned planes to ever fly and hands down the most advanced aircraft ever, relative to the tech available at their conception. We stand gawping for several minutes before photographer Dave – clearly a fanboy – starts spouting random, mind-blowing SR-71 facts. Listen up: the entire fuselage is a fuel tank, and because engineers needed to account for superheating and expansion of the titanium skin at cruising speeds, it leaked fuel through the panel gaps on the runway. The A-12, this crazy slice of reconnaissance perfection, was developed in under two years by a crack team of 135 engineers led by Kelly Johnson, and the SR-71 took flight a little over two years after that. This is significant.

Kevin Czinger claims he took inspiration from the SR-71 when he was devising the 21C – not for the styling or powertrain – but for the skunkworks mentality that made it possible to build a spy plane capable of cruising at Mach 3.2 at 85,000 feet in such an incredibly tight time frame. He wants his Californian hypercar, like this Californian plane, to be a giant leap, a tech reset that challenges everything we know about how we build cars. Except, as we've previously decided, the Czinger 21C might have four wheels and

078
SPECIFICATION

POWERTRAIN
ENGINE IS A 2.9-LITRE TWIN TURBO THAT MAKES 937BHP AND COULD REV BEYOND ITS 11,000RPM REDLINE

BODY
21C HAS NOVEL ONE-PLUS-ONE SEATING POSITION. COCKPIT CONFIGURATION HAS STRONG FIGHTER JET VIBES

STRUCTURE
SAY HELLO TO THE 3D PRINTED CAR. SUSPENSION, FRONT CRASH STRUCTURE, AND DASHBOARD ARE ALL MADE THIS WAY

DESIGN
THE UNIQUE MANUFACTURING PROCESS DICTATES THE 21C'S ORGANIC SHAPE. MORE OF AN EXO-SKELETON THAN A TRADITIONAL CAR

VEHICLE TYPE –
MID-ENGINED, REAR-WHEEL DRIVE COUPE

POWERTRAIN –
IN-HOUSE DESIGNED 2.9-LITRE TWIN TURBO, 937BHP V8, 550LB FT, TWIN E-MOTORS ADD 237BHP FOR A TOTAL POWER OUTPUT OF 1,174BHP @ 11,000RPM (1,332BHP OPTION AVAILABLE – THAT'S ALMOST 1 MEGAWATT OF POWER), AN AXIAL FLUX MOTOR GENERATOR UNIT, 4.4KWH BATTERY PACK

WEIGHT: 1,165KG (DRY)

DIMENSIONS –
LENGTH: N/A
WIDTH: 2,050MM
HEIGHT: N/A

TRANSMISSION –
SEVEN-SPEED SEQUENTIAL TRANSAXLE

PERFORMANCE –
TOP SPEED 281MPH (IN LOW DRAG SPEC)
0-62MPH 1.9 SECONDS
0-186MPH 8.5 SECONDS

079
BRAIN-FRAZZLING FACT(S):

THE SOFTWARE THAT HELPED DESIGN THE CZINGER 21C ENSURED THAT THE SILENCER DOESN'T JUST MUFFLE THE EXHAUST, IT ALSO ACTS AS AN INTEGRAL PART OF THE REAR CRASH STRUCTURE. THE 3D-PRINTED RECTANGULAR EXHAUST TIP HAS AN X MOTIF SO THAT IT CAN SPIT X-SHAPED FLAMES ON THE OVERRUN. THIS ISN'T JUST A NEW CAR, IT'S A NEW WAY OF MANUFACTURING CARS.

a windscreen but it isn't really a car at all, it's a demonstrator for what's possible with digital design and 3D printing.

Peer into the engine bay and it's more anatomy lesson than automotive tradition – sinewy, organic shapes looking like tendon and muscle bolted to simple off-the-shelf extrusions. The immediate benefits are obvious – putting material only where you need it reduces weight and builds strength – but it runs deeper than that. By 3D printing the gearbox casing, for example, you can integrate the heat exchangers into the internal structure, rather than hanging them off the side. And when you have complete flexibility in the size and shape of components you can print, there's complete flexibility in how you design and build that car with none of the costs associated with traditional car factories.

Driven by Kevin's love of superbikes, and his insistence on a one-plus-one seating layout, the proportions are extraordinary: it's long and low from the side then insectile from the front, with its two metre width cradling a sliver of a cockpit. Naturally, a front axle full of electric motors, a driver, a passenger and a V8 engine all in a line brings certain quirks. The position of the driver, pushed right into the nose like a Seventies turbo-era F1 car, is one; the world's longest dihedral doors are another. Not to mention the massively wide side sills (home to the twin 2.6kWh batteries) that you have to sit on and swivel to post your legs in.

Here we go then. Let's give ourselves a run up to pull out onto the road – a series of smooth curves and elevation changes we've picked out with generous turning circles at either end. The CEO, on the lookout for other cars, gives me the thumbs up. Release the brake, let it trickle forwards then ease out the clutch paddle with an unsympathetic side order of throttle. A stutter, but we catch it and we're up and running and wow, instantly, it's all about the central driving position. As in a McLaren F1 or Speedtail, it not only laser focuses you on the job of driving but makes placing yourself on the road an art form.

The data's flooding in. From the ride quality (surprisingly supple) to the gearbox (now as clinical as it was truculent at low speeds, smacking in upshifts so long as you're on throttle, banging down the gears with all the subtlety of a well-judged Anthony Joshua uppercut), the throttle response (some initial lag despite the electric assistance, giving way to a dam burst of torque as the turbos spool) to the steering (light, quick, but loading up properly in the turns). There's potential and promise here, no doubt about it, but we're not in its happy place. What we need, is somewhere to really throw the shackles off…

As we wait in the pits – strapped in, helmet on, feeling more than a little sweaty and fretful while a small army of mechanics mills around checking vitals – one of the more senior engineers catches our eye. He smiles, gives me a thumbs up followed by the unmistakable international sign – palms down pushing towards the floor – for breathe, stay calm, and if you crash this thing, I'm going to personally strangle you.

Message received, loud and clear. It's around this time our mind wanders to the car's recent achievement – this actual car – taking a two-second bite out of the McLaren Senna's lap record at Laguna Seca in the hands of Joel Miller. (In July 2024, the 21C will set a new production car world record up the hill at Goodwood, when test driver Chris Ward set a time of 48.83 seconds. Borderline insanity.) Today we're at Willow Springs and there shall be no lap records. Joel's here (it was him doing the shakedown when the roof ejected itself) but there simply isn't time to set up the car and give him a proper crack at another scalp.

Besides, there's some British journalist hogging all the seat time. A sighter lap of Big Willow, one of the oldest tracks in the US, confirms it doesn't take any prisoners – an endless double-apex right hander here, an off camber crest directly into a downhill right hander there, a mammoth straight braking into a 90° left… it's not a layout to be taking any liberties on when you've got well over 1,000 highly boosted horsepower at your disposal, no traction control and rudimentary ABS.

Gently does it for half a lap, then we can start attacking a bit harder. Immediately the ragged edges are smoother, the gearbox works better, the steering gets more talkative and the aero starts to work, pinning you down in the faster sections. The manners might need refining, but the fundamentals are solid. The more confidence we find, the car matches and multiplies it. It's up on its toes now, jinking and playing. The engine lights the afterburners on the straights, but prefers a lower gear and all the revs in the slower stuff (first gear runs all the way to 75mph). We're too used to instant torque these days, and this thing requires more flogging, but get it right and the results are predictably eye-popping. Out here, chasing lap times not traffic lights, is where the 21C was born to be and in a moment none of the false starts and mechanical hiccoughs matter. It's simply a privilege to be tearing up the track, chasing the embers of the day, in something as genetically advanced as this.

It's a mighty undertaking, this car, but the idea it represents and the inspiration behind it sets it well apart from the vapourware pack. There are flickers of genius here and a genuine road map to production, which is why we leave with ears ringing, hands tingling and a whole lot of hope.

Imagine what it'll be like when it's finished.

Brakes? We don't need brakes where we're going...

Aluminium, titanium, carbon fibre... the Czinger C21 is a material sciences laboratory on wheels

WHY IT'S HERE
Ferrari doesn't do retro but its Icona series is steeped in historical inspiration. And this is the best example yet

FERRARI DAYTONA SP3

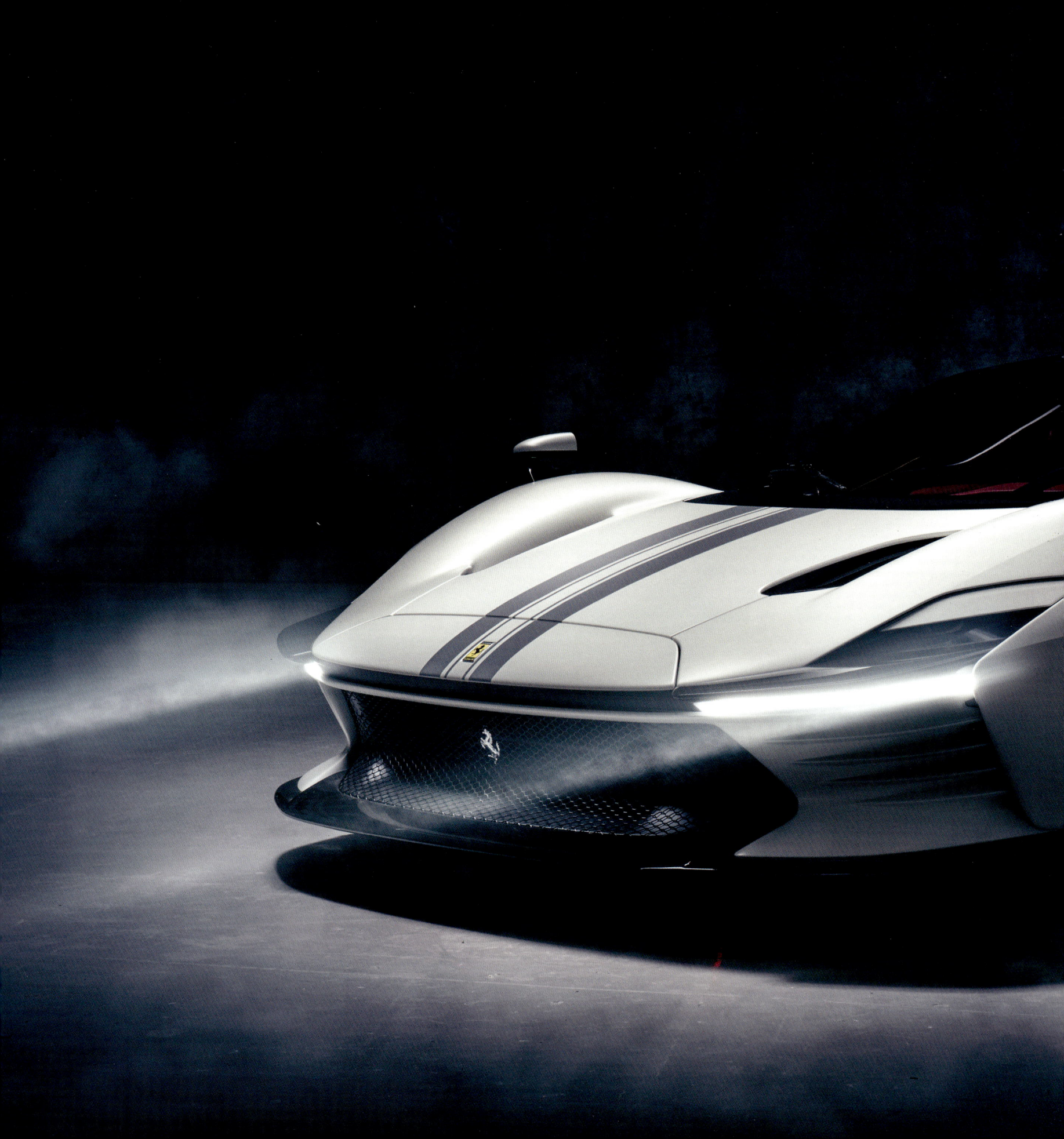

The temptation must be enormous, but Ferrari will never do a 'continuation' car. Enzo Ferrari had more pithy one-liners than your average stand-up comic and the best known is probably "my favourite Ferrari is the next one". Or words to that effect. The Old Man never looked back, you see, even in his dotage. But he also liked making money so he'd surely approve of the Icona series, a model line that allows Ferrari to peruse its back catalogue for inspiration while projecting forwards, future-focused ethos fully intact. Rest assured, there are no unallocated chassis numbers lying around in Maranello waiting for their moment in the sun. The past is a foreign country.

Now meet the Daytona SP3, a limited series, carbon fibre-bodied and mid-engined naturally aspirated V12 two-seater fuelled by memories of the spectacular late Sixties/early Seventies Sport Prototipo era, and the 1-2-3 result in 1967's Daytona 24 Hours race in particular. Ferrari will make 599 examples, each costing £2m. Owners of the inaugural Icona, the Monza SP1/2, were given first refusal on the new car, with an additional 100 units of the SP3 made available over that car's 499 production run to accommodate anyone who didn't go for its predecessor. It's also globally legal, unlike the roof- and windscreen-less and rather more compromised Monza.

There isn't a car design studio in the world that doesn't feature images drawn from that golden era of sports endurance racing. Porsche's 917 is probably the ultimate example of this epic sub-genre, but head 450 miles south from Zuffenhausen to the Modena area and Ferrari's contribution is incalculable. From the pontoon-bodied 250 Testa Rossa via the 250 GTO and 250 LM to the 330 P3/4 and 512 M, we're talking almost 15 years of endurance racing royalty. In fact, it isn't just the cars, it's the haircuts, sunglasses, and the entire typography of the era that's so seductive.

That finish in '67's Daytona race was memorably choreographed so that the three cars – a P3, P4 and 412 P – could take the chequered flag in unison. Payback, if any were really needed, for the rout Ferrari suffered at the hands of the Ford GT40 six months previously at Le Mans (a race Ferrari had dominated since the late Fifties, with six consecutive wins from 1960 to '65). Hence the new car's name, something that was hotly debated internally.

Why? Because a new Ferrari Daytona is obviously going to invoke the memory of the original Ferrari Daytona, the modernist masterpiece front-engined V12 GT that arrived in 1968, and whose Pininfarina-drawn visuals set the co-ordinates for an influential new design path. Except that it was never officially called Daytona, it's known instead by the more prosaic name 365 GTB4, and is a completely different sort of car (though it too was later raced successfully). "We think the name perfectly captures the Icona concept," Vice President for Sales and Marketing Enrico Galliera explains. "The result in Daytona was Ferrari's revenge on Ford."

Ferrari's Chief Design Officer Flavio Manzoni has long cited the 330 P3/4 as a personal favourite, but he's really gone for it this time. "I think this is the best car I've ever been involved with," he says. "It's a futuristic interpretation of a classic sports prototipo, and a perfect showcase for what

The Daytona SP3 cockpit is a sensational place to be. The seats are integrated into the chassis, which reduces weight and amplifies the competition car sensation. It also looks extremely cool

the team at Ferrari Centro Stile can do."

The cues are all there but magnificently mashed up. Where to begin? Look at it head-on and the cresting front wings are straight out of the classic endurance racing playbook, flanked on either side by a pair of functional bonnet air vents. The headlights follow Ferrari's current slimline LED path but have "eye-lids" that retract in a way that recalls pop-up headlamps. The door mirrors have been repositioned to the top of the wings, another emotive nod to the great endurance racers. And check out the "cab-forward" stance and the way the windscreen wraps around the cockpit, an effect heightened when the detachable roof panel is in place.

Then there are the "butterfly' doors, which feature an integrated air box that delivers air to the side-mounted radiators. There's a beautifully pinched waist, and an organic softness to some of the forms is matched by a genuine edginess elsewhere. That's not an easy trick to pull off. The rear might be the wildest part of all, composed of a series of horizontal blades that underscore the SP3's futuristic character while referencing a car that's more obscure than any of the other ghosts that haunt the new car: we're talking about Pininfarina's 1968 Ferrari 250 P5 concept. The tail-lights are set into a horizontal light bar beneath the spoiler; the tail-pipes exit through the upper part of the diffuser.

"You can take cues from the past but it's vital that you don't lose the visionary approach," Manzoni continues. "You can see how it's possible to connect the beauty of our heritage with our vision for the future. We would never

"THE DAYTONA SP3 CONNECTS FERRARI'S HERITAGE WITH ITS VISION FOR THE FUTURE"

Opposite, the Daytona SP3 manages to reconcile Ferrari's past, present and future. Few cars have this sort of presence or philosophy

do a restomod or make something that is banal or obvious. Because I'm a designer I have to be creative. I simply cannot accept the idea of just reproducing something that happened in the past. Nor are we held back by peoples' expectations of what a Ferrari should look like."

Manzoni, it seems, goes his own way. Technically, the Daytona SP3 is also intriguing. It's tempting to see it as an analogue LaFerrari, shorn of all the hybrid components that marked that car out as such a trail-blazer when it arrived in 2013 but which, paradoxically, now rather dates it. It's funny how things work out. We're pretty sure we're not the only ones who speculated and fantasised about a LaFerrari 'unplugged', but Enrico Galliera is very quick to scotch the idea.

"This is emphatically not a LaFerrari Speciale," he says firmly but with a steely smile. "When we do a new hypercar it's the pinnacle of performance, exploring a new technology frontier. The Icona model line is more design-driven, and we have some collectors who are very focused on that aspect of Ferrari. Although some elements are shared with the LaFerrari, the philosophy and strategy are completely different."

But while the Daytona SP3 effectively remixes some existing componentry, it's still as sharp as a blade. The chassis and bodyshell are made from carbon fibre composites, much of it derived from aeronautics and Formula One, including T800 carbon fibre for the tub and T1000 for the doors and sills. This is as good as it gets in the automotive context: in fact, it's so strong it's the same material used by the nuclear industry to make the centrifuges in which they enrich uranium. Gulp.

Note also that the seats are integrated into the chassis, as was the case on the LaFerrari, reducing weight, optimising the driving position and promoting a distinctly single-seater feel inside. It feels very racy indeed, to the point where anyone over six-foot tall or packing a bit of extra timber might struggle to get comfortable. The HMI is the latest Ferrari system; the main instrument display sits in a pod that almost floats above the carbon fibre main structure. This could well be the best Ferrari interior yet – focused, reduced and emotive. We love the way the driver seat's trim flows into the passenger seat and then continues around the entire cockpit. There's nothing else out there that feels quite like this car from behind the wheel. It's all highly functional yet manages to have an intriguingly abstract quality.

There's nothing abstract about its aerodynamics, however. Ferrari says the Daytona SP3 has the highest level of passive aero efficiency it's ever achieved, so Centro Stile didn't have to worry quite so much about incorporating appendages, wings or flaps. But it's still a world-class piece of aero-driven sculpture: there are flicks and ducts at the front, the waisted mid-section is reminiscent of the coke bottle form of an early Nineties F1 car, there are underbody vortex generators, and floor chimneys that optimise the airflow under the rear of the car. These were only possible because the

SP3 has shed the LaFerrari's batteries, and they help remove air from under the body and send it across the rear wing. The biggest challenge has been in delivering aerodynamic harmony across the body. The Daytona SP3 generates 230kg of downforce at 124mph, has a dry weight of 1,485kg, and a 44/56 front/rear weight distribution.

Finally, the engine, which is the magnificent 6.5-litre V12 as seen most recently in the 812 Competizione. It makes even more power here – 829bhp – and can rev to a scalp-tickling 9,500rpm; it has 514lb ft of torque. Note that this is the most powerful V12 Ferrari has ever created. The pistons have been redesigned, there are lighter titanium con-rods, a material called DLC (diamond-like carbon) has been applied to the piston pins to reduce friction, and the crankshaft has been rebalanced and is three per cent lighter. Sliding steel finger followers in its valvetrain improve gas flow and combustion, a technique used on the most powerful superbikes that's partly responsible for their razor-sharp throttle response. There are also variable geometry inlet tracts on the intake to maximise the might of the explosions going on in the combustion chamber. Ferrari hints that the Icona series could theoretically become a refuge for the normally aspirated V12 even as the legislation tightens up ever harder. Another reason to love it, although we shall see how that plays out.

The SP3 uses the latest 6.1 version of Ferrari's remarkable SSC software, incorporating the Ferrari Dynamic Enhancer for the first time on a mid-engined car to trim the yaw angle and sharpen cornering agility even further. Top speed is in excess of 211mph, 0–62mph done in 2.85 seconds, 124mph in 7.4 seconds.

It could have made the car faster, Ferrari admits, but that wasn't the aim. A refreshing admission. The Icona project also brings with it a certain degree of freedom, and the lower volumes permit some cool technical innovations. There is carbon around the rear of the car, for example,

that comes from Formula One, which can support higher temperatures.

The SP3's purity doesn't extend to a manual transmission, though, even if such a thing was possible on a car this powerful. That would have been nostalgic, Ferrari says, and the Daytona SP3 is clearly not an exercise in navel-gazing. It's also a car whose rarity and value may condemn it never to turn a wheel in anger. But luckily we have driven it. So what's it like?

DRIVING THE FERRARI DAYTONA SP3

To lift or not to lift, that is the pressing question as we exit La Source hairpin and hug the pit wall like an overly large concrete comfort blanket. Pros: the conditions (warm and dry), the car (a highly sophisticated V12 mid-engined Ferrari) and the race situation (we have the track all to ourselves). Cons: circuit knowledge (this is your correspondent's first visit to Spa), and driver talent.

The Pros have it. We shuffle an inch lower in the seat – simultaneously dropping the centre of gravity and hiding behind the binnacle. Downhill straight crashes into towering incline, left-right-left, it takes every ounce of concentration to ignore our rational mind and prevent the right foot from retreating. The front wheels track straight and true through Raidillon, the engine flexes its diaphragm on top of the hill and bellows a 12-gun salute to the memory of the endurance racers it keeps alive, and we're safely onto the Kemmel straight, just as a perfect finger of light reaches through the clouds to bless the SP3's passage.

Aaaand… all that occurred at 44mph. Shame. Ferrari's call not ours: "Due to the value of the car and the fact that it's a limited edition model, the maximum speed allowed on circuit is 70kph." Brutal. The deal was this: we got four hours to drive the Daytona SP3 with vigour on the roads around the Spa Francorchamps circuit, then two hours on one of the world's fastest racetracks, in one of the world's most exciting cars, at congested M25 speeds. Enough for a carefully curated photo call to fill in the back story of this car, not remotely enough to find the limits in a one-of-599, 828bhp psychopath worth £2m. Fear not, we learned about the fire in the SP3's belly on the road earlier and we'll get to that, but first a short history lesson.

Ferrari claims it doesn't do retro – you won't catch it knocking out any straight resurrections from the past like the, erm, reimagined Lamborghini Countach, but it is happy to reference its history. A lot. Which is where its Icona range comes in: "To distil the very essence of an era and use it as a springboard to create new concepts that become icons for future generations." This is the third Icona model (the first being the beautiful but largely pointless Monza SP1 and SP2 from 2018, yep, the ones without windscreens), and it represents Ferrari's homage to its impossibly glamorous sports prototype racecars from the Sixties.

Did we like the SP3 when we first saw images of it? The jury was out. The catfish front end, the puffed up front arches, the venetian blind rear… it felt like too much. It was trying to reference too many things while simultaneously insisting on being something unique and future facing – a noble aim, but ultimately a design cue, or 10, too many. Yet, staring at it in an unremarkable lay-by on a quiet Belgian B-road, you can't help but be floored by its magnificence, its drama, the sheer spectacle of it. For starters, it's ridiculously low and wide, something you're constantly aware of on the public road as a tractor scrapes past, without flinching, in the opposite direction. But then there are the details, and the thought poured into each of them, that you simply can't appreciate on a computer screen. The front is salvaged by retractable flaps that reveal the main beams. A modern take on pop-ups that should be made mandatory with immediate effect.

Then there are the intakes for the side-mounted radiators perched atop the butterfly doors, with an air channel running clean through them, leaving the waist section corseted and perfectly smooth. Rear wheel arches, wider than the fronts, fill the wing mirrors and melt majestically into a full width rear lip spoiler (despite 230kg of downforce at 124mph there's no active aero here, a deliberate ploy to keep the package period correct), that tips the stance forwards. High pipes leave space for more diffuser and, finally, the slats. Oh the slats. It's medically impossible to take your eyes off them.

094
SPECIFICATION

POWERTRAIN
ENGINE IS FERRARI'S NAT ASP 6.5-LITRE V12, WHICH PRODUCES 829BHP AND REVS TO 9,500RPM

SOFTWARE
DAYTONA SP3 IS THE FIRST MID-ENGINED FERRARI TO USE THE DYNAMIC ENHANCER TO TRIM THE CAR'S YAW ANGLE AND SHARPEN HANDLING

BODYWORK
CHASSIS IS MADE OF T800 CARBON FIBRE; DOORS AND SILLS USE SUPER-STRONG T1000 CARBON

AERO
FERRARI SAYS THE DAYTONA SP3 HAS THE HIGHEST LEVEL OF PASSIVE AERO EFFICIENCY IT HAS EVER ACHIEVED

VEHICLE TYPE –
MID-ENGINED, REAR-WHEEL DRIVE COUPE

POWERTRAIN –
6.5-LITRE, 829BHP V12, 514LB FT @ 7,250RPM

WEIGHT: 1,485KG (DRY)

DIMENSIONS –
LENGTH: 4,686MM
WIDTH: 2,050MM
HEIGHT: 1,142MM

TRANSMISSION –
SEVEN-SPEED DUAL CLUTCH AUTOMATIC

PERFORMANCE –
TOP SPEED 211MPH
0-62MPH 2.85 SECONDS

BRAIN-FRAZZLING FACT:

THE CARBON FIBRE USED IN THE DAYTONA SP3'S CONSTRUCTION IS THE SAME GRADE AS THE MATERIAL THAT'S USED BY THE NUCLEAR INDUSTRY TO MANUFACTURE CENTRIFUGES. THOSE ARE THE BITS OF KIT THAT THEY USE TO ENRICH URANIUM, SO YOU CAN IMAGINE HOW ROBUST THEY HAVE TO BE. IT'S ALSO THE SAME LEVEL OF CARBON FIBRE THAT SCUDERIA FERRARI MAKES THE FORMULA ONE MONOCOQUES OUT OF.

"They're repeated in the front intakes for a reason," Adrian Griffiths, Ferrari's Birmingham-born designer explains. "It's as if they run through the car, like a stick of Blackpool rock."

Let's dive in shall we? The butterfly door swings up and out, taking most of the sill with it, leaving a bare-bones view of the carbon tub you're about to post your backside into. And just to head off rumours nice and early – yes this is an all-carbon, mid-engined, V12 supercar much like the LaFerrari, but this is not simply an LaF with the hybrid bits pulled out. That chassis had to accommodate batteries behind the seats and an e-motor so a straight copy/paste wouldn't have made sense. Griffiths describes LaFerrari as much more of a road car, how you sit on it rather than in it. He also points out that the visibility line is 40mm lower than on the SP3, the seating position slightly less reclined. You sink into seats attached directly to the tub then draped in Alcantara that flows over onto the sills and centre console. Looks uncomfortable, is anything but. The windscreen bends around you, so you sit deep in the car's guts. Pull the wheel towards you, slide the spring-loaded pedal box around and it fits like a glove. The overall driving position and feeling of enclosure isn't far off the effect achieved in the Sixties endurance racing original.

Want to see the sky? Five clips and the targa roof lifts off, but we leave it on because there's drizzle in the air. Not ideal when you've got the 812 Superfast's magnificent naturally aspirated V12 behind you, albeit uncorked further with upgraded internals – like titanium con rods – for even more power. In fact, this is the most powerful engine Ferrari has ever fitted to a road car, which focuses the mind. It also now revs to a screaming 9,500rpm, the same red line as the 812 Competizione. Sure, it might lack the LaFerrari's

"THE V12 PICKS UP VIVIDLY AT 3,500RPM WITH A LINEAR SHOT OF VIOLENCE"

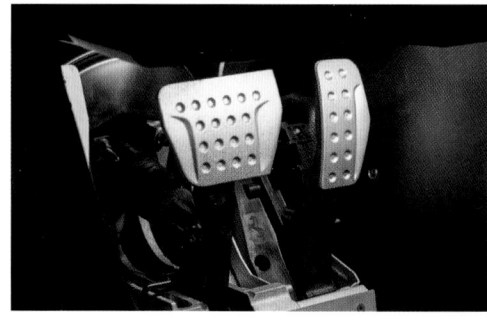

Right, from the butterfly doors to the distinctive body slats, the Daytona SP3 dares to push the boundaries

986bhp e-assisted knockout punch, but 0–62mph in 2.85secs and 211mph (almost identical power and performance figures to the more affordable V6 hybrid 296 GTB, stat fans) isn't exactly shabby.

There's still no substitute for 12 pistons, untainted by turbo or electricity. This engine rips, picking up properly around 3,500rpm with a linear shot of violence straight through to 9,500rpm, by which point you're both breathless and travelling a wee bit fast. The sound is special – a bassier intake warble from inside the car with the roof on, but a shrieking wail of decibels to anyone lucky enough to be in the vicinity. That engine, this gearbox, it's the supercar powertrain perfected. And for a car that lists Le Mans winners among its greatest influences, it's not nearly as harsh as you might expect. Dial the manettino up to Sport or Race, engage bumpy road mode and on the road it's a sharpened blade with a comfort handle. Yes, you get gravel rattling around in the wheelarches and collecting on the sills, no it wouldn't be a joy to parallel park, but if you don't mind buying a toothbrush and T-shirt when you get there, big big miles are there for the taking.

The steering is as hyperactive as you'd expect from a modern Ferrari, but some noticeable extra weight has been dialled in as a nod to the high-living Sixties. Despite driving away from a gaggle of execs, engineers, designers and mildly concerned PRs very gently, a few hours later we're lobbing it about and using every last rev because this is a car designed to be grabbed by the scruff of its neck. Forget the fact it's Surrey mansion money, you're driving a 458 Speciale on anabolics.

Best bit? You don't need to be on a quali lap to enjoy it, because it's infused with Ferrari's secret sauce that manages to make 800+bhp feel approachable, friendly even. Thanks to electronic wizardry the chassis is always on top of the engine, and this driver is mostly on top of it all. You might have to be very high up in Ferrari's little black book to be invited to drop £2m on one, but it's not a members' only experience, it isn't aloof, it actually democratises elite performance.

Overzealous speed restrictions or not, to be given the opportunity to drive a Daytona SP3 is a sizeable privilege. But the thrill isn't the price or the rarity, it's the execution. Ferrari's most powerful ever engine, with the correct number of cylinders unfettered by electricity, placed behind the driver then surrounded by carbon and electronics that feel totally natural. It's about as pulsating as it's possible for a car with a numberplate to get, and Ferrari at its very best… even at 44mph.

 **6**

WHY IT'S HERE
It takes everything that made the McLaren F1 so mind-blowing and *improves* it. Could this be the greatest driver's car ever made?

GMA T.50

Join us as we scoot across into the centre seat of the Murray T.50. It's much easier than in the McLaren F1 because the carbon fibre main chassis spars no longer frame the centre seat. So sit backwards on the high sill, pivot around, slide your feet across flat floor into footwell, wriggle bum over and drop down into cupping seat. You'll now give an involuntary sigh. There are several reasons for this, the least of which is the small bit of physical exertion you've just undergone. Above that is the sense that you have plugged yourself in and the fit, the driving position and sculpted seat are all perfect.

And it's then that the symmetry of it all hits you. From the BAC Mono to the McLaren Speedtail, a central seat is just better. It seems to soothe the brain. Usually at this point some killjoy likes to scoff and point out something about French toll booths. Get a blipper or Telepass. Any more for any more? OK, yes, the border control at Eurotunnel. The fact they can easily see you through all the glass probably won't wash. At least it ensures the cabin is light and airy, complementing the clean, simple design.

Now look more closely, because there are stories to tell. And Gordon Murray is telling them. Most of them include the word kilogramme. Gordon's sitting in the T.50, we're kneeling at the door (worshipping at the altar, basically) and today's reading is taken from the book of pedals. "I did the stress calculations for the pedals, and I said to the designer, 'look at the F1 pedals, but you won't get them any lighter.' But then I decided to have a go too, and I realised that the anti-slip you need for the regulations could be the sharp edges of the metal. As a result these are 300g lighter."

There's a lot to unpick here, not least that the car's overall architect, now well into his eighth decade but with energy to spare, can't leave a single element of the car alone. There's an enthusiasm about Murray, about his quest for engineering perfection, that's as infectious as it is impressive. And like all car brands that have a messianic figure at their head (see also Horacio Pagani and Christian von Koenigsegg), the car reflects the man.

But wait. Those front and rear badges are clearly enamel, not a lightweight solution. So where else has he let the odd gramme creep in? "Nowhere," says Murray, followed by a detailed explanation of the badge's design and how it was impossible for enamel to be used more thinly. Gordon points around the cockpit: the titanium gear linkages save 800 grammes, the substrates under the trim are 3D printed for precision and weight saving, the chassis plate ahead of the gearlever (it's actually being sent out to buyers in a presentation box) is 4.5mm thick so looks heavy, but has been milled out to just 1mm thick from the back, so it weighs just 7.8 grammes. And now, as you can read, we're dealing in tenths of a gramme.

Weight is a major thing on the T.50. Or the lack of it. We know how much each headlight pack weighs (2.1kg, including the heat sink and the fan needed to cool it), that the Arcam hi-fi, with amp, 10 speakers and 700w of power is just 4.3kg – half the weight of the Kenwood system in the F1. Gordon had given them a target weight – no, that's wrong – a maximum weight of 5kg. Like, we suspect, every other supplier involved in the Murray

Although the GMA T.50 is a car of high performance and equally high drama, it's also easy to see out of and to operate. Because these things really matter when it comes to driving incredibly quickly

103

Left, you notice the dihedral doors first. But GMA is equally proud of the T.50's headlights. Below, the engine is a 4.0-litre naturally aspirated V12, which can rev to 12,100rpm in its most extreme mode. Pin back your lug-holes…

T.50 project, they'd initially baulked at the challenge, before realising that this project would be a great shop window and learning exercise. But there's so much more here than an obsession with weight. As Murray puts it, "Everything is engineering art." He couldn't find cockpit switchgear without play in it, so he went to a military aeronautics firm to do it. He loathes touchscreens – "they shouldn't be allowed in fast cars, trying to jab at a screen is absolutely ridiculous," – so small, simple clickwheels on the steering wheel control the screens either side of the central rev counter. No fancy graphics dancing on those either ("it took a lot to hammer that home with the supplier"), just simple, clear, white on black information.

Then there's the rev counter. Do you remember when Lexus launched the LF-A and said that the dial had to be digital because a mechanical needle couldn't keep pace with how fast the engine revved? The LF-A's V10 was truly amazing, able to flash from tickover to the 9,000rpm cutout in just 0.6secs. When Gordon set out the engine parameters with Cosworth, there were two main stipulations. Neither of them was a power or torque figure. No, what he asked for was an engine that revved high and revved fast. He wanted it to rev higher than the Light Car Company Rocket, and faster than the F1. Both are cars he designed. No car has ever revved higher than the 11,500rpm Rocket; vanishingly few – the LF-A being one of them – have matched the F1's capacity to pile on over 10,000rpm a second. Just let that sink in…

"IF THE McLAREN F1 IS YOUR NORTH STAR, THE T.50 UPDATES AND IMPROVES EVERY ELEMENT OF IT"

Murray loves small capacity Sixties Italian V12s, so based his initial calculations on a 3.3-litre. It's now 4.0 litres, but that hasn't harmed its appetite for revs. It'll reach 12,100rpm, and get there from rest in 0.3secs. A gain rate of 28,400rpm per second. Twice as fast as an LF-A. Imagine what's going on with the titanium internals. Ponder how much more exciting that is than learning the T.50 is just another 1,000bhp supercar.

It's mid-afternoon before Gordon mentions that it has 664bhp and 353lb ft of torque, and even then only in passing as he's more animated about the fact that they have 71 per cent of that available at only 2,500rpm, 6,500rpm below the peak. "That's the bit I don't understand," he explains. "How they play off injection against torque with ignition timing. And my goodness the thermal side of the engine is so clever. Cosworth must be the best engine company on the planet." These are the claims: the world's highest revving, fastest responding, most power dense, and lightest naturally aspirated V12. Gordon can't help adding that "there's nothing in common with the [Cosworth-developed Aston Martin] Valkyrie V12, this is really the next generation on." And the dial that encapsulates all of this for the driver? "Of course the rev counter is mechanical."

And the gearbox is a manual. No need to ask why. It's an open secret that supercar design is basically Top Trumps: cars are designed around numbers, chiefly speed numbers. Power, max speed and 0–60 sell cars. That, nearly as much as ease of use, accounts for the shift to twin-clutch gearboxes. They are quicker, so the numbers are better. Gordon Murray still hasn't got a clue what the T.50's 0–60mph time will be. Well, he can probably guess it to the nearest hundredth of a second, but he's just not interested. What he cares about is delivering the most immersive driving experience possible, and as you will know if you've ever driven a Tesla Model S or a Citroen 2CV, speed and fun are very separate things. The gearbox is an H-pattern manual from motorsport specialist Xtrac, which has supplied half the F1 grid.

"It'll have the best shift action of any car," says Gordon, before going into detail about crossgate angles ("only nine degrees when typical cars are 15"), ratio choice and how they can adjust feel into and out of each slot. Tell him that the finest manual we've driven belonged to a Honda NSX Type-R and he is open in his appreciation for it. "I copied the NSX for the F1," he says. "It was very clever, they sped the cable up so there was never any slack in it."

Here's what else is notable. Suppliers. Gordon wants the T.50 to be a rolling showcase of British engineering. And more by luck than judgement, this extends to the toolkit. Famously, the F1 had a Facom titanium toolkit. Facom is French, but Gordon got in touch for the T.50 "and the guy was English, and said 'Would you come to head office to discuss it?' I said, 'Certainly, whereabouts?' and he said 'Slough'. Turns out Black and Decker has bought Facom, so it's a British company."

You won't be wondering why the McLaren F1 figures so strongly in this story and you won't appreciate quite how similar they are until or unless you have the opportunity to walk around the side of the T.50. The window line is similar, and behind that, the familiar slender, upright, single seat. Parked together, Gordon comments how much neater and cleaner the T.50 looks.

He's right, but it also lacks the F1's visual drama. Famously, there are elements of the F1 that Gordon didn't like, compromises he had to make. "The spine is 50mm too wide, the headlamps are like glow-worms in a jar, the aircon was hopeless, the brakes squeak, the clutch needs adjusting every 5,000 miles, the fuel tank bag replacing every five years, loading luggage in the lockers was a pain."

It certainly hasn't been easy creating the T.50. "I was prepared to pull the plug when I heard McLaren was doing a three-seater," and some of the engineering challenges have been huge. "No one really cares about steering any more because it's so difficult. It drives you insane… but I've got perfect geometry." It's not power-assisted, but clutches in some assistance below 10mph to help parking. The system is patented. The storage lockers are in the same place ahead of the rear wheels, but now accessed from above via two huge butterfly wing-style engine covers. There's 30 litres of storage around the cabin.

And most obviously, there's a fan in the back. Did you know there were two fans in the F1's diffuser? They improved high-speed stability, but the T.50 makes them look like leaf blowers. Downforce isn't the main aim here. Instead Gordon talks of centres of pressure, stabilising the rear to shave 10 metres off the 150–0mph stopping distance. There are six different modes, "the funkiest is Streamline, where we shut the valves to the floor, drop the wing angle to minus 10 degrees and pull air from the engine bay. That gives us a 12.5 per cent drag reduction."

The GMA T.50 is an insanely, intensely fascinating car. Only 100 will be made, each costing £2.36 million plus VAT. "But it's not £20 million [like an F1]," says Gordon, "so I point out to customers this is a car that delivers the same experience, but better in every way, and with an 80 per cent discount." Will the T.50 make the same leap in value? That depends on its legacy – which could be potent. As its creator comments, "It's got a good chance of being the last great analogue hypercar."

DRIVING THE T.50

Ever since we started driving, we've been looking. You may not realise you've been looking, but you have. The trouble is, you'll never find it. Well, we've found it now. The NA-137. The GMA T.50. The road. And the car. And that's it. Here's what we'd do with that final tank of fuel.

We don't know whether to feel relief or profound excitement that Gordon Murray and his team have created arguably the finest driving device ever conceived. No less was expected after all. And yet, despite everything we'd already learned about it, this wasn't the car we expected it to be. It wasn't better or worse, it was just different. This wasn't a 'one road' thing, by the way. The T.50 was ours for four whole days and close to 900 miles. The length of the Pyrenees, from Barcelona to Bilbao. We knew it had potential, but hadn't expected it to throw up the Driving Nirvana Combo. Just a road trip, really, but what a road trip, taking in about 25 cols and passes, investigating the length and breadth of this secluded mountain range, ricocheting between Spain, France and Andorra. The stuff that lights our fires. More importantly, the stuff the GMA T.50 was designed for.

A point on that: this is not your common-or-garden hypercar, is it? In fact, you could argue it's not a hypercar at all considering it's got less power than an entry-level McLaren Artura. Gordon says "It's all about honouring and improving the F1," and there's a lot to discuss there. It's certainly a breath of much needed fresh air, compared with the existing hypercar hierarchy, all those Bugattis, Ferraris, Koenigseggs and Paganis which are rolling artworks, glorious self-promoters and vanity display cases all rolled into one. Many of them are mesmeric to drive, but that's not the focus. In fact, driving feels like a job they've outgrown in their quest for impact. I suppose that gives them a broader range of talents than the T.50, about which the most accurate sobriquet is probably "the driver's hypercar".

"SO MANY HYPERCARS ARE GLORIOUS SELF-PROMOTERS. THE T.50 IS ALL ABOUT THE DRIVING EXPERIENCE"

Because really, that's all you want to do with it. The rest is a glorious by-product.

This is a ruthlessly optimised car. No power steering. No twin clutch gearbox. No touch-screens. No adaptive dampers. A Sport mode that adjusts nothing but the throttle. No turbos. No wings. What you're left with is a three-seat cockpit in a rear-drive carbon tub, powered by a naturally aspirated V12 engine, the whole thing weighing less than a tonne. That's right, 997kg as it sits here. Most rivals are at least 50 per cent heavier. What are they doing with all that weight-saving carbon? What's exotic about the T.50 isn't the artistry, but the engineering itself.

We meet it parked up at GMA's service centre in Barcelona. Its compact neatness is disarming – it's no more intimidating than a Porsche Cayman – but it has a few tricks. Press and hold the unlock button on the overly chunky key and all doors and engine covers rise together, an enticing piece of choreographed drama. We load it with stuff we'll need for the next few days, finding places for wallet, cap, sun cream, phone and water bottle, plugging in USB leads, fitting bags into bays. Bigger stuff goes in cubbies under the passenger seats, smaller stuff in magnetically lidded ones either side of the dash. Everything is within easy reach. There are no cupholders, because as chief engineer Nik Hoyle explains, "There are two things Gordon loathes above all: rear anti-roll bars and cupholders."

Time to get in, a process we imagine is a bit like being a gymnast on a pommel horse – your hands have to support your weight and move you across the cabin, while your feet merely scurry across the flat floor. The pedals and steering wheel can be adjusted with spanners, the carbon seat slides and has interchangeable foam panels that adjust the shape and firmness. It feels instantly good. It's the perfection of the position, the slender rightness of the circular steering wheel, the latticework pedals, the gearlever's stark simplicity, the clarity of the instruments and layout. There's no fanfare, just an anticipation of operation. And for what lies ahead. If the McLaren F1 is your automotive North Star, remember that the T.50 is Gordon Murray's idea of updating and improving it. It's impossible not to feel some trepidation.

Barcelona beckons. Slide your index finger under the light, almost fragile starter button cover. Short presses start things, longer ones stop them. A short press and the V12 bursts into life. Only that's not the engine, it's the integrated starter generator, a 48V system that does the heavy lifting of spinning the crank before it fires so it needs less fuel, starts more cleanly. After a few seconds of ISG action a *bam-uhhh* that makes everyone jump announces the engine has not only fired, but instantly settled into its idle.

To get rolling smoothly don't touch the throttle – the revs will only zing and fizz. Instead just lift the clutch, let it start engaging and only then use the right-hand pedal. Feel its weight and precision beneath your foot. Realise, as you go for the shift back into second, that it's all going to take a bit of learning when the movements are this crisp, short and mechanical. But wow, the instant sense of connection.

A bit of power steering is clutched in at low speed, but above 10mph you're on your own so there's weight to deal with there as well. But really the first thing that strikes you is how manageable and useable it all feels. Again, there's no sense of intimidation when you're surrounded by so much glass and have such intuitive switchgear. Montjuic is swarmed with other learner drivers but we soon feel comfortable progressing, so head north on smooth, quiet motorways. There's a deep intelligence to the GMA T.50.

You wouldn't describe it as smooth and quiet, though. The anticipated semi-GT vibe based on its lightness, a daintiness, and eagerness to scamper along like an Alpine A110 doesn't materialise. It's more stiffly sprung than expected, taut in its movements, and there's constant road hum. Knocking along at 2–3,000rpm is where you detect similarities with the larger Cosworth V12 in the Valkyrie – both share a plain mechanical thrash of pure engine noise. So excessive in the Valk that you need ear defenders, here it's way, way calmer. Easily overcome by the 700w Arcam stereo, and doesn't dominate a cabin chat or a phone call either. There's nothing here to prevent long-distance use, as the first toll booth approaches.

It's the first reminder that the driver sits in the centre. It comes so naturally, the symmetry soothes the brain. The toll tag soothes the path through. No need to wiggle a hand out the window slot. Borders are crossed, into France, then Andorra, with equal ease. The cadence of driving has picked up with the elevation, hints of savagery lurking as the needle ventures further around the central dial. So much more to go, though. This is a car you build up to, that doesn't reveal its secrets all at once – there are so many facets to indulge and appreciate, it comes across as sensory bombardment. Everything, if it's not chattering away, is providing tangible satisfaction.

Here's an example. You approach a roundabout, trying not to fluff the downshifts because the car deserves better; you check directions on the

CarPlay and marvel once again at how well that integration is done; you check the mirrors and note the camera screens are exactly where they need to be; you indicate and appreciate how simple the process is when the steering wheel is shorn of all frivolity; you note how glorious it is to position the car when you're sat centrally; the steering loads up and you delight in that even at modest speeds; and as you twist the lock off you remember why you wore race boots to drive it: because the throttle pedal looks so good, has been designed to perform to its best, that it deserves the best of you, too.

What we're saying with all of this is that it's not just the tangible driving stuff that stands out here. Other cars celebrate the engine or the chassis. The T.50 celebrates *everything*. And because it gives you so much satisfaction, you respond to it not as a machine, but something more human. Up and over we go at Pas de la Casa for a day and a half of playtime across the Col de Cabus and Port d'Envalira – at 2,408m, the highest pass in the Pyrenees. A little factoid for you here. Thanks to gravity, stuff weighs less at altitude – up here the T.50 is just 996.966kg. That's right, we've saved 34 grams. You're welcome, Gordon.

The engine doesn't notice any oxygen deficiency. It's an absolute wonder, this Cosworth V12, the best road car engine we've ever used. Not for what it does at 12,000rpm – that's just the headline everyone focuses on – but for what it does everywhere else. We can burble through villages in fifth ("The speedbump-to-180mph gear," Nik tells us) because of how tractable and smooth it is at 1,500rpm, before surging the throttle between four and 5,000rpm because of the intake pulse and gargle. But really it's all about 6–9,000rpm, because that's where the containable magic happens: response, torque,

energy, crescendo, leaping charisma and a compelling, addictive, *snarl*.

And it's containable for a reason. Beyond 10k the propulsion is so vivid, so wild, so nerve-jangling, it's all you can do to keep your foot down. The noise now is pure Nineties F1 scream. So much information is coming at you that you struggle with the processing. Everything – road, traffic, visibility, surface – needs to be aligned when you pin it at the top end. Those opportunities only present themselves a couple of times each day. Good. It makes them even more special when the stars do align.

The noise, apparently, reverberates so accurately off distant mountains that on a couple of occasions the video team are convinced there's more than one T.50 in the vicinity. Perhaps the villagers will be out with pitchforks when we crawl through, but because the T.50 is small, because it isn't a bewinged, beslatted aggressor, we're forgiven. We head south and west from Andorra, chasing sunset along the N-260. Look it up. Many bikers proclaim it the world's greatest road. It dances through Pyrenean foothills, into

The T.50 is similar in size to a Porsche Cayman, so driving it on a normal road isn't the nerve-shredding experience it is in some hypercars. It's useable, accessible

112
SPECIFICATION

ENGINE
HEART OF T.50 IS A 4.0-LITRE NATURALLY ASPIRATED AND REV-HUNGRY V12. IT'S UNBELIEVABLY RESPONSIVE

DESIGN
CENTRAL DRIVING POSITION AND LOW COWL MEAN THAT THE T.50 IS EASY TO PLACE ON THE ROAD AND SEE OUT OF

BODY
CARBON FIBRE MONOCOQUE AND BODY PANELS TOTAL LESS THAN 150KG. THIS IS AN AMAZINGLY LIGHT CAR, WHICH AIDS AGILITY

AERO
THERE ARE SIX DIFFERENT AERO MODES, INCLUDING A LOW DRAG ONE. THE MAIN AIM IS TO MANAGE THE CENTRES OF PRESSURE ON THE CAR RATHER THAN GENERATE DOWNFORCE

VEHICLE TYPE –
MID-ENGINED, REAR-WHEEL DRIVE COUPE

POWERTRAIN –
4.0-LITRE NATURALLY ASPIRATED COSWORTH V12, 664BHP @ 11,000RPM, 353LB FT @ 8,000RPM

WEIGHT: 997KG (DRY)

DIMENSIONS –
LENGTH: 4,352MM
WIDTH: 1,850MM
HEIGHT: 1,164MM

TRANSMISSION –
SIX-SPEED MANUAL GEARBOX

PERFORMANCE –
TOP SPEED 226MPH (WITH SHORTER 6TH GEAR)
0-62MPH NOT KNOWN BUT LIKELY TO BE SUB-3.0 SECS

113
BRAIN-FRAZZLING FACT:

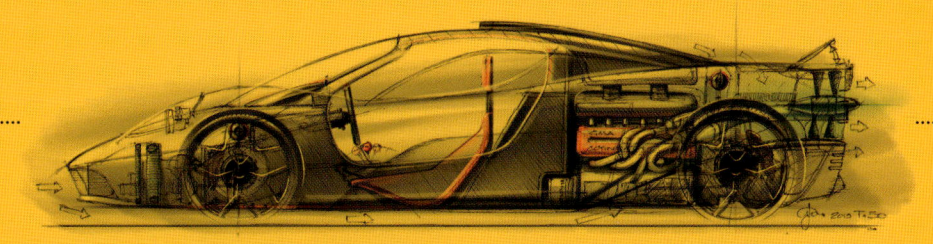

THE T.50'S GEARBOX IS SUPPLIED BY F1 AND MOTORSPORT SPECIALISTS XTRAC. IT WEIGHS JUST 80.5KG AND FEATURES A 184MM TRIPLE PLATE CARBON SILICONE AND TITANIUM CLUTCH. GMA TRIED THREE DIFFERENT GEARLEVER WEIGHTS TO GET THE ACTION EXACTLY AS THEY WANTED. DESPITE THE RUTHLESSLY WEIGHT-OPTIMISED METHODOLOGY THAT GOVERNS THE ENTIRE CAR, THE CHOSEN ONE WASN'T ACTUALLY THE LIGHTEST.

gorges, over cols, on tarmac laid with love and absent of traffic. It's often narrow, the sort of place hypercars fear to tread. Not when they're only 1,850mm wide. Again and again this is what strikes you about the T.50: how easy it is to use, how rewarding it is in everything it does.

It has a sweet spot though, and that's in third and fourth gear corners. The steering weights up a lot through hairpins, making it physical to drive. It'll make your shoulders and triceps ache, along with backache from the seat. The vertical headrest is a strong signature when you look through the car, but it might prove too upright for some. But such issues disappear through sweepers, using the mighty Brembo stoppers, building up speed and confidence. The harder you go, the better it gets. It wants to be driven with proper inputs: heel and toeing is best when you've got some actual travel into the brake pedal, the gearchange – so tight, so precise, so controlled – wants to go through fast or the revs drop almost to nothing. That third/fourth plane is a delight, the shift itself not the slick flick of a Civic Type R, but something heavier, more connected and mechanical. Something you'll enjoy attempting to perfect. A lifetime's work.

Everything starts to come to you. Up until now it's occasionally been frustrating because it doesn't suffer foolish inputs, it doesn't fluff your ego. It demands accuracy and effort. But now the magic of the suspension is revealed. You feel everything, all loads, all surface grumble, yet nothing throws the T.50 off balance. Composure is complete. You don't want it softer now, this is the Goldilocks set-up, compliant enough for

motorways, and sharp enough for track use. Who needs adaptive dampers?

It's night time when we get to Pamplona. The headlights have proven to be yet another boon – no matrix LED trickery, just a precisely edged block of potent main beam, activated by the left paddle. We trickle the T.50 into the pedestrianised centre at midnight. Width restrictors? No issue. Big speed bumps? Likewise. Gordon would never condone nose lift, not when you could do the ground clearance and overhangs correctly in the first place. And fit a couple of surreptitious nylon scuffpads just in case. The T.50 doesn't make too much impact among the arm-in-arm strollers until the doors flare open. Everyone is intrigued, few know what it is, but those that do almost fall over themselves. This is another part of the GMA's appeal.

Dawn. La Piedra de San Martin is deserted. It's also utterly fabulous. It's earthier, more remote and tucked away than a Disneyland pass such as the Grossglockner High Alpine road in Austria. It was clearly constructed by artists, artisan road builders who appreciated the need for an unnecessary tunnel, a climbing loop, a journey through rocks and trees, a tease and crescendo of scenery. Nik Hoyle joins us in the passenger seat and we giggle and gasp at the sheer perfection of it.

To be fair, the journey here is spectacular from 50 miles out, and by this stage we're fully in tune with the T.50. It's not for everyone. It's more demanding to drive than we'd expected because it's raw, pure and unfiltered. That last is the word that keeps coming up. Because that's what sets the T.50 apart from every other hypercar in this book. They all filter the experience, send signals through electric processors, reducing your connection while increasing their capability. It's clever stuff, of that there is no doubt, and this cleverness allows them to travel faster but airbrushes the experience.

The T.50 is the slowest fast car we've ever driven – and simultaneously the fastest feeling. This is reductive engineering at its finest. It's not just the weight loss, it's the removal of everything that interferes with driving. The result taps more deeply, intuitively and rewardingly into your driving centres than any road car of our experience, as if your hands reach down past the physical controls. Total immersion. And yet there's more to learn. Another reason we'd have it for a last-ever drive – to know there's more to discover.

"THE T.50'S GENIUS IS IN ITS REMOVAL OF ANYTHING THAT INTERFERES WITH THE DRIVING"

#7

WHY IT'S HERE
No longer the eccentric newbie, this Swedish outfit has earned its place at the top table via terrific design and technical innovation

KOENIGSEGG JESKO ABSOLUT

"The Jesko" **BANG** "Absolut is the latest and" **BANG** "greatest hypercar to come from" **BANG** "the sizeable mind of Christian von" **WU-BUP-BUP-BUP-BANG** "Koenigsegg." Cut there, let's go again…

Delivering a simple line to camera in anything with a healthy amount of horsepower, under full acceleration, is an acquired skill. In the Jesko, it's pretty much impossible. It's not the ferocity of the g-force squeezing me against my seat like a giant potato masher that's the problem, I can cope with that, it's the ninja reflexes required to click the upshift paddle before colliding with the rev limiter that's proving tricky. So we keep going, run after run, until my brain, eyes, ears and right hand are sufficiently recalibrated, a perfect launch is in the bag, and my adrenal glands dangle like shrivelled walnuts off my bruised kidneys. Brilliant but exhausting.

To be fair, there are some typically revolutionary pieces of technology here that are conspiring against smooth human performance. The first is a gearbox, a new nine-speed 'Light Speed Transmission' that blows raspberries in the general direction of a twin-clutcher. Essentially you have two sets of three gears that compound to create nine possible ratios – like a bike derailleur system – with the first three extremely closely stacked (hence the repeated headbutting of the rev limiter), the next three a bit more spaced out, and the final three further apart still. Yes, it is rather complicated.

It features six individual clutches for the forward gears and a seventh for reverse, so all gears are constantly engaged and ready. And the benefits are

If you had almost 1,600bhp under your right foot, you too would look like this. The Koenigsegg Jesko Absolut demands respect and restraint. Most of all, it demands an empty runway

Koenigsegg has followed its own path for three decades now, marrying high technolgy with extreme design – and it's all done with a dash of humour

Left, not so much a gear-lever as a portal to a whole new world of automotive high performance

many. Not only are shifts, quite literally, bang on, you can also jump from one gear to any of the others. It's also smaller and two-thirds the weight of a comparable nine-speed box. Plus, and here's the real kicker, it means the engine doesn't need a flywheel, so it has a demented appetite for revs, like a 1,600bhp superbike.

The engine is a flat plane crank 5.1-litre twin turbo V8 that for the most part gives naturally aspirated sensations and always feels extremely angry indeed. It produces a maximum of 1,578bhp and 1,106lb ft of torque, can rev from idle to 8,500rpm in 0.2 seconds, while 0–62mph takes around 2.5 seconds and top speed in this slightly softer and more slippery Absolut version is theoretically the scary side of 310mph. Theoretically, because no one's found the space, or summoned the nerve, to find out yet…

Only 125 will ever be built, costing around £2.3m each, but then the spec is the stuff of breathless teenage dreams. We're talking carbon bodywork, carbon tub, hollow carbon wheels (weighing less than 7kg per corner), carbon ceramic brake discs clamped by in-house designed calipers (Christian isn't interested in buying in anything he can make better himself), and a total weight of 1,390kg dry – 30kg less than the stiffer, bewinged Jesko Attack. There's 1,000kg of downforce at 171mph in the Attack version, but that drops to 150kg on the infinitely cooler looking Absolut we've got to play with – identified by its rear fins instead of wings, less aggressive front splitter and carbon inserts on the rear wheels to more effectively cleave the air. Except one of them came loose on our first full-bore run and was munched by the wheel, so exposed spokes it is.

Beer and fast cars. That's why we're here. Unequivocally two of my favourite things, and yet to my eternal frustration, two pleasures rarely enjoyed together. But where there's a will, there's a way. The plan, in our traditional style, could have been spat out by a computerised feature generator. We are in Ängelholm, Sweden, on a mission to deliver Jesko beer to Jesko von Koenigsegg in a Koenigsegg Jesko. Try saying that fast five times after a plate of pickled herrings and several digestifs. Wordplay to one side for a moment, there was method to the badness.

Jesko beer, brewed locally, made its world debut at the 2019 Geneva Motor Show, when the Jesko car also got its first airing. And back in 1992 when Christian was a young man with distant dreams, making his money flogging frozen chickens to the highest bidder, Jesko von Koenigsegg was instrumental in getting Koenigsegg Automotive off the ground. He helped to secure a startup loan and pledged three to four weeks of his time to assist Christian set up in a small town in the southeast of Sweden, called Olofström. He was still there five years later working 18 hours a day.

Fair to say Jesko's unwavering generosity hasn't gone unnoticed and culminated in Christian naming his latest and greatest hypercar after his dear old dad – a fact he kept secret from him until the press conference at the show. No, *you're* crying. As tributes go, it figures because the Jesko represents everything Koenigsegg stands for: beauty, excess, usability, craftsmanship, engineering bravery and raw, bloody-minded performance. Nobody does it the way these guys are doing it.

We're standing on Koenigsegg's runway turned testing strip, just a few minutes drive from the factory, trying to absorb the opulence and detail in this carbon-fibre bullet. Even photographer Mark and videographer Dave, who'd normally be weeping gently on first sight of dark grey and naked carbon bodywork on account of its light-sapping superpowers, are making ooohs and ahhhs as they circle it. It pulls off a trick of being, proportionally, hypercar 101, but with its softly curved snout, pinprick headlights and visor-like glass, it couldn't be mistaken for the product of any other company. Again, nobody does it the way Koenigsegg does, and we love them for it.

Blip a button on the key fob and the doors flip forward automatically – a piece of theatre that refuses to wear thin – drop into the carbon-shelled bucket seats and you're surrounded by an interior that's fairly sparse – mainly a portrait screen in the dash, a couple of cupholders and lots and lots of carbon fibre. There's an instrument screen attached to the steering wheel that stays level even as you wind the lock on – reeks of a gimmick, actually works brilliantly – and there's more space for two people in here than any

The Absolut's engine has 1,578bhp and 1,106lb ft of torque. Yet the car itself is the slightly softer and slippier version of the Jesko

"THE 5.1-LITRE TWIN TURBO V8 ALWAYS FEELS VERY ANGRY INDEED"

The Jesko Absolut is so much more than a car that can accelerate very quickly. It bubbles with sensation and feedback

Koenigsegg that's gone before. Then, just as we fire the engine and sit there listening to the saw-edged idle, it starts to rain. Turns out cold Michelin Pilot Sport Cup 2s, outrageous amounts of power and a wet track make Jack a dull boy – we retreat to a trailer for hot tea and await dryness.

Good decision because once we're back out there, it's unhinged. We're talking five-star, unfiltered, mind-scrambling shove all delivered without lag to an explosive, serrated soundtrack and with the subtlety of a donkey kick to the side of the head. And then I discover we're running on standard super unleaded, so I have only 1,262bhp (for the full 1,578bhp you need to fill it with E85), and spend the next hour trying and failing to think of a situation where you could realistically use 300bhp more. This is one of life's more arcane questions, admittedly. I ask one of the engineers what it's like juiced up on E85. "Like having nitrous boost, constantly."

But acceleration alone isn't a party piece these days, not when EVs have turned straight-line speed into a cheap commodity. The Jesko's true genius reveals itself slowly, in the light steering that crackles with information and the predictability of the brakes. In the accessibility of its performance and its sense of humour. Want to toast some tyres? The Jesko has no interest in putting you off – the merest hint of squat under throttle,

dive under braking and roll into the corners helps you feel out the limits of grip, then as you step over them it's all balance and lightness. This isn't a garage ornament, it's a car you could, and should, use regularly and thoroughly.

And so we do, swapping closed runway for public highway. Heading north from the factory through sweeping rural B-roads – marvelling at the fact that this 300mph missile can do docile, too – to the town of Båstad, or bastard as we, the British contingent, insist on calling it. This starts something that's hard to stop because a large number of Swedish words appear to be twinned with British toilet humour. We buy some lunch at Willy's, drive past Bad Cok and see several signs reading "Infart". I'm only just regaining my composure when we pull over for fuel – a process that involves lifting (hydraulically, no actual effort is required) the entire rear clamshell like a

SPECIFICATION

POWERTRAIN
THE 5.1-LITRE TWIN TURBO V8 IS MATED TO A 'LIGHT SPEED TRANSMISSION' THAT HAS TWO SETS OF THREE GEARS

ENGINE
THERE'S NO FLYWHEEL SO THE ENGINE CAN REV FROM IDLE TO 8,500RPM IN JUST 0.2 SECONDS

BODY
JESKO ABSOLUT IS A RIOT OF CARBON FIBRE – BODY, CHASSIS, THE WHEELS. A CAR AND A PIECE OF ART

AERO
JESKO ABSOLUT HAS LESS DOWNFORCE THAN THE MORE EXTREME ATTACK VERSION BUT STILL LOOKS MIGHTY

VEHICLE TYPE –
MID-ENGINED, REAR-WHEEL DRIVE COUPE

POWERTRAIN –
TWIN TURBOCHARGED, 5.1-LITRE V8, 1578BHP
[ON E85 FUEL], 1,106LB FT @5,100RPM

WEIGHT: 1,390KG [DRY]

DIMENSIONS –
LENGTH: 4,845MM
WIDTH: 2,030MM
HEIGHT: 1,210MM

TRANSMISSION –
KOENIGSEGG NINE-SPEED 'LIGHT SPEED' TRANSMISSION [LST]
WITH GEARBOX CONTROL MODULE

PERFORMANCE –
TOP SPEED 310MPH-PLUS [THEORETICALLY]
0–62MPH 2.5 SECONDS
0–186MPH 13 SECONDS

PRICE:
£2.3M

BRAIN-FRAZZLING FACT(S):

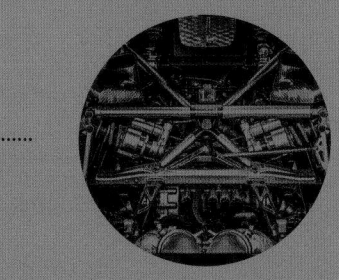

THE JESKO ABSOLUT'S TRANSMISSION USES SIX INDIVIDUAL CLUTCHES FOR THE FORWARD GEARS AND A SEVENTH FOR REVERSE. THE SHIFTS ARE INCREDIBLY FAST BUT IT ALSO MEANS THAT THE DRIVER CAN JUMP FROM ONE GEAR TO ANY OF THE OTHERS. THERE'S NO FLYWHEEL, SO IT HAS AN ASTONISHING APPETITE FOR REVS. IN MANY RESPECTS IT FEELS AS RESPONSIVE AS A SUPERBIKE – ONE THAT HAS ALMOST 1,600BHP.

peacock, which does tend to attract every camera phone within a two-mile radius. If you're an introverted billionaire who doesn't live in the wilderness, you have been warned. This one might not be for you, after all.

Then we get the call – Jesko, who lives in Stockholm and is 83 years old, has travelled south for five hours and is happy to meet us at a Koenigsegg family friend's house nearby. We arrive just as the light's fading and crunch up the driveway towards a sizeable country pile. The door swings open and there he is, all smiles and waves, perfect English and infectious energy. Before we sit down he wants me to hold his jacket so he can sit in the car – I offer to assist, but he gently bats me away. We photograph him in the driver's seat, grab a couple of coldies, then head inside to crack our… oh… zero alcohol Jesko beers. The boozy ones were out of date apparently. Oh well, it's "quite drinkable" says Jesko, and he has to drive anyway. As do we.

We sit soft in the library, clink glass and learn the correct pronunciation of "skål", then I listen to Jesko's story. How Christian had "a lot of interests and a great number of friends growing up." How Christian presented him with a business plan with "everything from A to Z, I was rather impressed." How in the early days he would phone Christian who was in the workshop 500 metres away and he'd say, "Father, please don't disturb me, I'm building the car." How for Christian "nothing is really good enough" and how he's "been to the Geneva show, every year for 20 years, and people always ask me, 'how come it costs that much?' It's just a car with four wheels? My answer is sorry, 'but this is not a car. It's a piece of art.'"

In these unsettled financial times, an air of greed and gluttony follows supercars and hypercars around. These are machines that find themselves fighting harder than ever to earn their place in society. Nobody needs something like this, but Koenigsegg always finds a way to stay the right side of uncouth. It's the purity of Christian's vision, I think – to build the best hypercar the world has ever seen – that hasn't wavered or warped with fashion, and his refusal to compromise, ever, that creates something far beyond just a car. It really is a piece of perfection, and in the Jesko it also gains an emotionally charged back-story. We'll drink to that.

"KOENIGSEGG'S VISION HASN'T WAVERED OR WARPED. THE RESULT IS BEYOND BEING JUST A CAR"

Right, one of these objects costs £2.3m. The other is a large house in the country. Below, engine, suspension and chassis are all highly functioning pieces of art

WHY IT'S HERE
Recreating an Eighties icon like the Countach? Good luck with that. And yet Lamborghini has taken a brave pill and jumped right in

LAMBORGHINI COUNTACH LPI 800-4

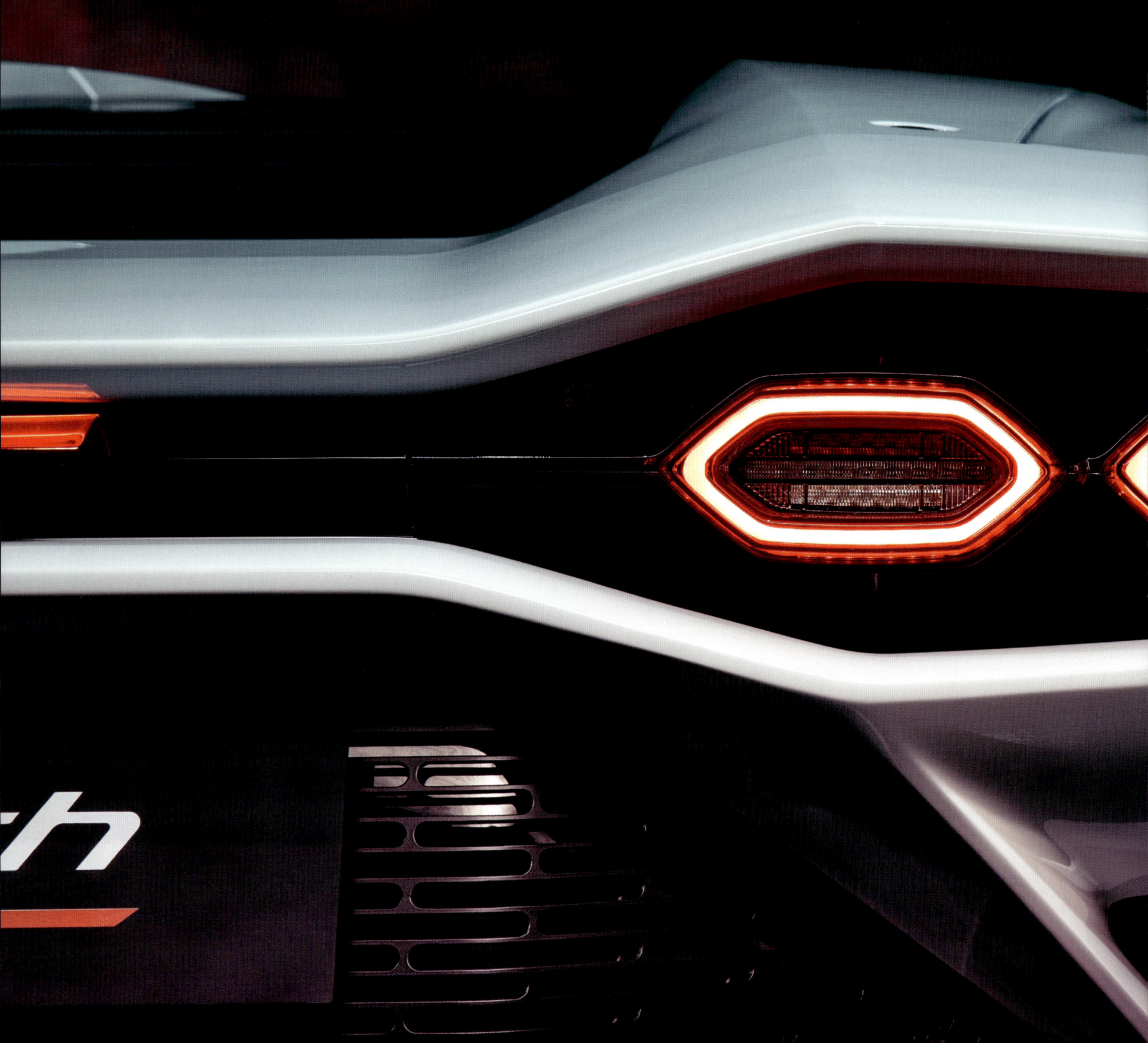

"THE WORLD'S MOST FLAMBOYANT CAR MAKER HAS GONE BACK TO THE SOURCE"

Above, Lamborghini Countach LPI 800-4's retro/not retro design fits right into an Eighties vapourwave context. Below, Design Director Mitja Borkert's sketches trace the evolution of that epochal shape across the generations

The Lamborghini Countach LPI 800-4 posits the idea that the world's greatest supercar had never ceased production, evolving instead through model cycles to rock up 50 years after its shocking debut looking like… this. Only 112 will be made – referencing the original's LP112 internal codename – costing north of £2m each, and they've all gone. But of course.

Anniversaries are easily won excitement generators and irresistible money spinners. Sant'Agata has been here before, of course. The Countach bowed out in 1989 with an actual Anniversary edition, although that car was celebrating the company's 25 – mostly turbulent and always fascinating – years in the game (the car itself was a mere 18 at the time). Horacio Pagani was the man who dared to reframe the epochal original, an act akin to daubing a moustache and little round glasses on the Mona Lisa.

Less well remembered is 2006's Miura concept, a 30th anniversary reimagining of the car that kick-started the whole mid-engined supercar thing in the first place. Walter de Silva did that one, but Lamborghini and its then-new boss Stephan Winkelmann evidently weren't feeling it. Half a century, though, is a substantial chunk of time, and both 1971 and the Lamborghini Countach are worthy of committed celebration. The Sixties changed everything, but it wasn't until '71 that the new decade announced that things were going to be different round here, musically and culturally.

Left, no matter how hard it tries, the 'new' Countach can't replicate the disruptive impact of the early Seventies original. Instead it acts as a 774bhp love letter to arguably the wildest looking hypercar of them all. Ducts, slashes and intakes galore

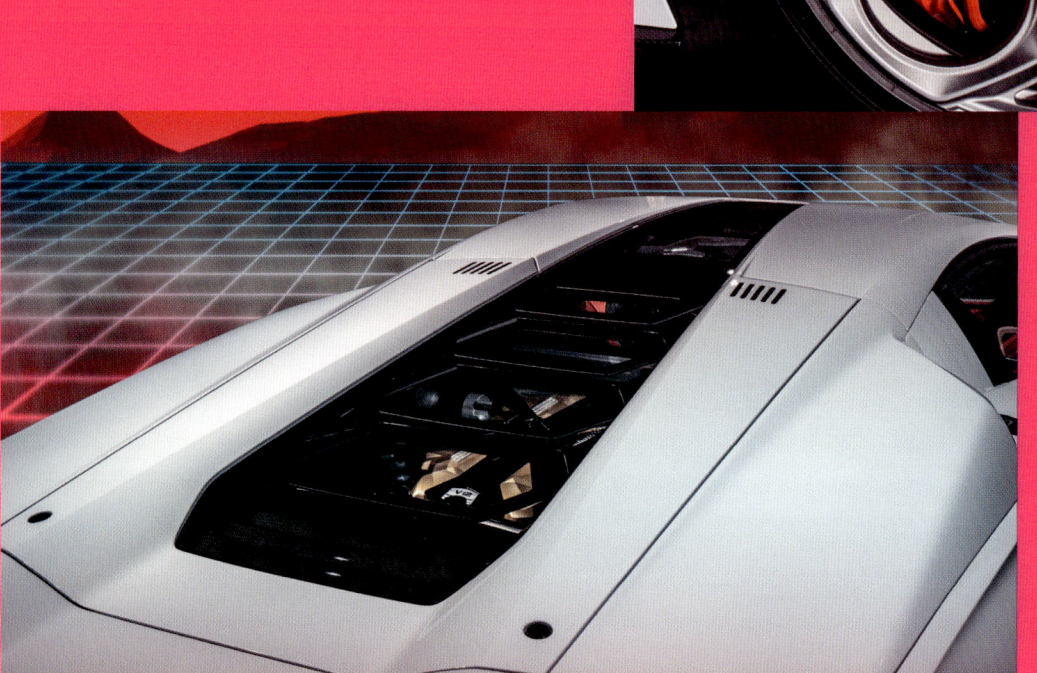

Left, the heart of the matter. Countach LPI 800-4 is powered by an angry-sounding 6.5-litre V12 augmented by a 48V e-motor

Meanwhile, in Turin a car designer called Marcello Gandini had spent much of the previous five years rehearsing his moves before setting the controls for the heart of the sun with '71's Lamborghini Countach LP500. If high performance Italian cars had previously dedicated themselves to a notably sensuous form language, things were definitely changing. You get the impression that Gandini would have made the wheels hexagonal if only that hadn't defied 5,500 years of engineering evolution. Instead, he did the next best thing and ensured the wheelarches were acutely angled, along with the rest of the car. The trifling matter of being able to see out was dealt with by introducing a periscope – *periscopio* – in place of the rearview mirror. The channel it carved into the Countach's roof would become a signature element. As did the infamous scissor doors, the only solution on a car as wide as this but another masterstroke.

However, designing a car like this is one thing, building it quite another. And this is where Lamborghini stunned the world by actually putting Gandini's UFO into production. "Earlier in the Sixties there was the Porsche 911 and the Jaguar E-type," Lamborghini's Design Director Mitja Borkert explains animatedly. "We were coming out of the post-war aerodynamic design ethos and into something truly cutting edge. Especially in Italy. The big names were fermenting a design revolution but the Countach was the only one that became a reality. This is another thing that makes it so special."

Borkert grew up in communist East Germany so was denied the full schoolboy poster-on-the-wall Countach experience. In fact, the first Gandini-designed car he remembers seeing was the Citroen BX. A cool thing in its own right, especially in a sea of Ladas, but no Countach. Seven years into the job of running Lamborghini's Centro Stile, Borkert now knows every millimetre of every car the company has ever made. But none more than the Countach. "You can keep looking at it and never get tired," he says. "The original was the culmination of that four-year period that resulted in the Alfa Romeo Carabo, the Bizzarrini Manta, Stratos Zero and Maserati Boomerang. We were going to the Moon, Concorde was in development, there were student uprisings in Paris and Prague. There was a lot of revolutionary thinking, and cars acquired a lot of hexagonal shapes and powerful graphics."

Now Mitja and his team are risking the wrath of that corner of the internet that a) loves to reimagine hero cars and b) wastes no time abusing a carmaker if it goes there itself. This all-new 50th anniversary Countach is a risky enterprise and a reputation killer in the wrong hands. Fortunately, disaster has been averted. Weirdly, given its inspiration and the brand behind it, it's a masterpiece of restraint, a homage that builds out on the original's key elements without tipping into pastiche or, worse, appearing to be retro. Yes, once you know it's a Sián underneath, you can see a bit too much of the donor from some angles, but look at the flat plan of the nose, the asymetric rear wheelarches, and the way the ducts behind the side windows keep faith with the ultra-controlled surfaces of the original.

This is closer to the original than the later bewinged and more tumescent iterations, the ones that corrupted themselves for the coked up, big hair, metal-loving Eighties. It's taut, tight and looks terrific. Its full name is Countach LPI 800-4, and its technical spec will be familiar to anyone acquainted with the recent Sián hypercar. In actual fact, this isn't a new car but another run-out for the hard points that underpin the Aventador. The engine is a 6.5-litre V12 that produces 770bhp, aided and abetted by a 48V e-motor that throws another 33bhp and 26lb ft into the mix.

So the 'I' part of LPI stands for 'Ibrido', indicating Lamborghini's first steps on a journey that will eventually culminate in full electrification. Lamborghini goes about things its own way: this hybrid uses a supercapacitor rather than a conventional lithium-ion battery. So while a supercap can't store as much energy as a normal, equivalently sized battery, it has three times the power density and can also charge up pretty much instantly. Which makes it the best solution in the new Countach, where the motor's power and the energy harvested under braking is used primarily to torque-fill during gearchanges. This is an area in which the Aventador's fun but gnarly single clutch sequential box has never done its best work, and we know from our time in the Sián that the e-motor helps. It sits between the engine and gearbox, and weighs just 34kg. The chassis and body panels are made of carbon fibre, for enhanced structural integrity and lighter weight.

We doubt that anyone signing on the dotted line for a 50th anniversary Countach will be persuaded by its hybrid tech, though. This is all about bragging rights. But it also very deliberately reins in the showbiz.

"ALTHOUGH THE COUNTACH IS ABOUT BRAGGING RIGHTS, IT REINS IN THE SHOWBIZ. UP TO A POINT..."

Opposite, although related to the Siàn and the Aventador, the Countach cabin is still hi-tech. And very dramatic

"The Countach went through a lot of versions during its life, although fewer than 2,000 were made, so the idea was to have a clean, solid and timeless design for this one," Lamborghini CEO Stephan Winkelmann says. "We wanted to highlight the best elements, the squared off wheelarches, the quad exhaust, the air intakes, and the amount of tyre that's visible at the rear. We didn't want to overload the car. This is a pure celebration of something that happened 50 years ago. As a rule I don't like retro cars, I prefer to have a forward-looking vision. But the original didn't just change Lamborghini's DNA, it changed everything in the world of super sports cars, so this is a valid exercise. The Countach is always the reference car."

So it's modernist rather than madcap. It's also worth noting Mitja Borkert's form in this regard: during his time at Porsche he authored the magnificent Mission E (the Taycan's conceptual precursor) but was also responsible for the 917 Homage. This is a guy with an amazing knack for riffing off a company's greatest hits without coming off like a tribute act. "I couldn't and wouldn't go straight to this," he confirms. "We created cars like the Terzo Millennio first. The Siàn was a car for a concours event, where you take a glass of Prosecco and walk around the car and think, 'Do I like it? Do I not like it?' It was intended to be a car with a lot of flavours inside, like a very complicated wine. The Siàn is spectacular, it's part of the continuum that gave us the Veneno and the other limited run cars. I know full well that some people don't like it. That was part of the plan. But here I said to my guys, 'Now I want the clean car that everyone is expecting from me.'"

The NACA duct has grown significantly, Mitja admitting that getting air into the engine was the biggest challenge of all. "Just as it was for Gandini," he smiles. But while he admires the Quattrovalvole, the new car's movable rear wing is preferable to an outsized fixed aero appendage. The drama of the original's cut-off rear is repeated on the new car, including the quad exhaust pipes. The *bianco siderale* colour of the show car references Ferruccio Lamborghini's personal Countach LP400 S but includes some metallic blue elements for more depth. Inside, the car gains an enlarged multi-media screen and 3D printed air vents, while the cabin is finished with a very Seventies square motif. There's even a little button marked 'Stile design' which displays the design DNA of Lamborghini. Fortunately, there's substantially more room inside than in the comically cramped original, though still nowhere to put your mobile phone. Speaking of which, the alloy wheels use the "telephone dial" design motif. Overall, it's a highly sophisticated piece of work, all the more so because it was completed as Italy's COVID lockdown began and the team worked remotely.

"The Countach is the ultimate game changer," Mitja concludes. "I recall seeing one during Pebble Beach on Highway 1 and you could identify it from a mile away. The Countach went out of production in 1990 but I always had the feeling there was unfinished business, that the perfect Countach was not there yet.

"The NACA duct on the LP400 was a bit of an add-on. I love the QV because the wheels and wheelarches got wider. The Anniversary was a bit too much for me. So yeah, unfinished business. I wanted to do a car that was super clean and puristic. There's just one line on the front wing and we wanted to play with big surfaces at the rear. I'm more than happy to play around with those different shapes on the different cars we have. The Essenza is a 5.5m long racing projectile. The Siàn is a car that is beyond design. But the Countach is pure sculpture."

DRIVING THE COUNTACH

The wind has picked up again, the cloud is closing in. The weather changes 20 times a day up here on the Stelvio Pass. Earlier, when the rain lashed down and there was no shelter, we took refuge in the Berghotel Franzenshöhe behind us. We were lucky someone was in. A chubby marmot scampers across the rocks just above us, breaking our reverie. "I must get back," Stephan Bauer, Director of the Stelvio Pass, says. "Remember we are doing some resurfacing between 32 and 31." We tell him that's fine, we're mainly going to be working upwards, into the lower numbers. So, this is Lamborghini's new Countach. Swing the door up, slide down into the tiny blood-red cabin and just sit there, looking out, taking in the same view of painted

"THE COUNTACH HOWLS ALONG THE STRAIGHTS, SOUNDING TRIUMPHANT AND MAGNIFICENT"

peaks, dark rock, snow and the faint zigzag evidence of human activity through a windscreen so flattened it's more a skylight.

The framing is important. Driving up here earlier Matt Monro went on the audio system and the anticipation of what lay ahead was so intense it's all you can do not to choke up. Because the Stelvio Pass is closed. There's just us and the cocaine-white wedge, and we've got one of the most remarkable, unlikely roads on the planet to call our own. On days like these, indeed. Thumb the starter button and there's a brief screech from the starter and 12 cylinders yelp rowdily into life. The air's already thin here, up at 2,188m, so the naturally aspirated 6.5-litre gasper isn't going to be developing the full 770bhp. The e-motor won't be impeded at all, but that's a mere 33bhp, used to smooth out the gearshifts. In our experience of it so far, smooth is not the word we'd use to describe the sequential manual gearbox.

However, with power spread between all four wheels, each wearing a winter tyre, it's not like we've rocked up to climb the north face of the Eiger in snorkelling gear. More like overkill really. And if it all goes terribly, terribly wrong higher up, there's a full carbon monocoque and plenty of airbags. The pass here rises in stages, pairs of hairpins punctuated by longer straights that carry you further into this high valley towards the end game – the last 14 hairpins. They rise up a slope of profound, precipitous steepness.

As drivers we take the road for granted, as it see-saws at 10° up a slope of 60°: take the road away and it's hard to imagine how anyone ever thought it could be done. Blame Napoleon. Although he was mainly throwing his weight around elsewhere in Europe, his activities made the Austro-Hungarian empire realise it needed a land route between its main power centres in Vienna and Milan. West of the Stelvio was Switzerland, and to the east impassable glaciated valleys. A road in the shadow of the mighty Ortler mountain was the only option. Construction started in 1819 and took six years. It's not really a road, more a smooth roof laid over towering stone columns, cathedral-like buttresses and supports.

The Countach howls along the straights, revs soaring through third, finding its sweet spot, the sound triumphant, confident, magnificent, an engine given space, if not air, to breathe and making the most of it. It's audible over huge distances, but still somehow lost, a faint pinprick of noise from far away. Fun to listen to, if there was anyone to hear it. Inside it's incandescent. Yes, it wants more atmospheric pressure, but hey, even if 770bhp is more like 600bhp up here, who cares when there's a proud, gregarious V12 gargling and churning and leaping about behind you?

Half that would still be too much for the Stelvio Pass. It's tight, bumpy, the rock faces are intimidating (but not as scary as the stone balustrades and the fresh air beyond them), and the Countach is having to work hard. It suffers most on those final 14, the diffs hiccoughing around the hairpins,

SPECIFICATION

ENGINE
NAT ASP 6.5-LITRE V12 MAKES 770BHP. IT'S ASSISTED BY AN E-MOTOR THAT ADDS 34BHP, HELPS SMOOTH OUT SHIFTS

HYBRID
THE E-MOTOR SITS BETWEEN THE ENGINE AND GEARBOX, AND WEIGHS JUST 34KG

DESIGN
ALTHOUGH IT'S BASED ON THE SIAN, THE NEW COUNTACH DOES A GREAT JOB OF REFERENCING THE WILD ORIGINAL

AERO
COUNTACH HAS A MOVEABLE REAR WING, ALTHOUGH AN OLD SCHOOL FIXED REAR WING MIGHT HAVE BEEN MORE FAITHFUL

TECH
COUNTACH USES A SUPERCAPACITOR RATHER THAN A LITHIUM ION BATTERY. HAS BETTER POWER DENSITY

VEHICLE TYPE –
MID-ENGINED, REAR-WHEEL DRIVE COUPE

POWERTRAIN –
NATURALLY ASPIRATED 6.5-LITRE V12, 770BHP @ 8500RPM WITH 48V E-MOTOR AND SUPERCAPACITOR (34BHP), 531LB FT @ 6,750RPM

WEIGHT: 1,595KG (DRY)

DIMENSIONS –
LENGTH: 4,870MM
WIDTH: 2,099MM
HEIGHT: 1,139MM

TRANSMISSION –
SEVEN-SPEED GEARBOX WITH 'INDEPENDENT SHIFTING RODS'

PERFORMANCE –
TOP SPEED 220MPH (LIMITED)
0-62MPH 2.8 SECONDS

BRAIN-FRAZZLING FACT:

THIS LAMBORGHINI HYBRID USES A SUPERCAPACITOR RATHER THAN A CONVENTIONAL LITHIUM-ION BATTERY. ALTHOUGH IT CAN'T STORE AS MUCH ENERGY AS A NORMAL, EQUIVALENTLY SIZED BATTERY, IT HAS THREE TIMES THE POWER DENSITY AND CAN ALSO CHARGE UP PRETTY MUCH INSTANTLY. WHICH MAKES IT THE BEST SOLUTION IN THE NEW COUNTACH, WHERE THE MOTOR'S POWER AND THE ENERGY HARVESTED UNDER BRAKING IS USED TO TORQUE-FILL DURING GEARCHANGES.

the ride unyielding at these low speeds, the gearbox shunting from first into second, traction light flashing as wheels lift around corners. But the experience of it? Alive in the brain for years to come.

Time to head back down. Speed builds more easily, that's for sure. The first hairpin is a reminder to not only get all the braking done before the slope angle changes and the splitter graunches, but to slow with enough time and space to get the sluggish nose lift up. But it's more than that – at 4.9m long, 2.1m wide and with ground clearance that just allows the toe of a hiking boot to slip under the splitter (they were a mistake, horrible on the hair trigger throttle), you have to take the widest possible line around every hairpin. Not likely to go down well if you did have to tackle oncoming traffic.

We do have obstacles to deal with though. Once or twice on the way up, I have to get out and move rocks from the road. That had us glancing nervously up through the photochromic roof panel (it's meant to mimic the original Countach's periscopo arrangement), and pressing the button to turn it opaque – best not to see the impact coming. Now there are new rocks. And you don't want to be stopped for long in a £2 million hypercar somewhere there's evidence of freshly tumbled boulders.

Six to eight weeks, that's how long it takes to open the Stelvio. Rock clearance is pretty much the last thing they do – and not just from the road. They rope people up and walk them down the rock faces, kicking loose any rocks that might fall. Can you imagine? We come to a halt after hairpin 31. There's a massive trench across the road, four feet across and six deep. It wasn't there this morning. Smiling workmen jump from diggers and beckon us across the metal sheet. It's not thick, and you can picture it bowing like a wobble board, but our load barely deflects it. Held breath explodes from our lungs.

Too soon. At hairpin 32 the tarmac is so hot and freshly laid that recent rain is steaming off. Once again, people with mischievous grins urge us forwards. We drop the window and hear the tyres peeling off the tacky surface. Just below that we have to squeeze through a gap alongside the road-laying machine that actually has the men in orange wincing and giving delicate hand signals. Having run the roadworks gauntlet we drop below the lower barrier. The road is technically open here, where the Stelvio is at its darkest, roughest and tightest. Thick pines lean in, the road picks its way through, weaving in and out of view as if in a fairy tale. Trafoi, the first village you come to, is rich with history. The Bella Vista hotel at hairpin 46 is the original start line for the hillclimb, the first race held in 1898 and won by a Daimler. By 1935 when the Alfa Romeos of Tadini and Nuvolari went head-to-head, they were climbing the 46 hairpins, 9.1 miles and 1,446m of vertical in a little over 14 minutes. Come here, drive it and you realise how shockingly fast that still is.

The next morning we treat ourselves. With the key to the barrier in hand, we do a full run from the bottom to the top at dawn. It's as epic as you imagine, the noise, the bubbling steering, views opening and closing, tarmac scudding underneath, the vibration, pomp and raw charisma. Yesterday we learned that you really need to be in Sport mode; in Strada the gearshifts are too slow and the stability intervenes; in Corsa the ride is much too stiff. But still this is a hypercar looking for space to properly stretch itself. Then we discover that the key that operates the bottom gate also fits the top…

And 10 minutes later we're among pristine open snow fields. The Bormio side isn't as iconic, but as a road to drive it's vastly superior. More open and flowing, fewer hairpins, better surfaces. The Countach opens itself up, tears onwards. It's by no means a modern hypercar: underneath it's pretty much identical to the Sián, which had an awful lot in common with the decade-old Aventador, but age and tech have only served to magnify its shock value. It's not ashamed of itself, that's for sure. The occasional car appears. The owners of the shops and cafes, coming up to prepare them for the road opening. An old Passat approaches. An arm with a cigarette at the end drapes out of the window, motioning us to stop. There's no waving arms or cries of "*Bella macchina!*", all he's interested in is the fact it's 4WD and has winter tyres. He should have asked about fuel consumption. It's terrifying, and causes range anxiety. We've had to bring jerrycans.

We need to talk about the car. The original was a revolution; it defined not only the Seventies, but also set the supercar template we know and love. Lambo says this car is it if it had evolved, but no, the Countach was, and still should be, the ultimate disrupter. It should have been a leap, a new direction. The Countach should not be a Sián wearing some half-hearted design cues.

But that is to misunderstand the business of cars. Retro rules right now. Take 112 old Aventador chassis and turn them into £224m? Stroke of genius. Ah, but what about the harm done to the original's reputation? If anything it'll boost values, make people realise the place that car holds. The LP5000's wing would have looked good on it and it's not a great driver's car either – the gearbox is clumsy, the chassis borderline brutal. But then the Stelvio Pass, the famous flank at least, isn't a great driver's road. But that's the side you really want to drive again – and we'd rather do it in the Countach than a Ferrari SF90, a McLaren 765LT or any Porsche 911. Because what bonds them is their shared drama, scale and glory. Lamborghini Countach on the Stelvio? At this altitude it's literally a match that's made in heaven.

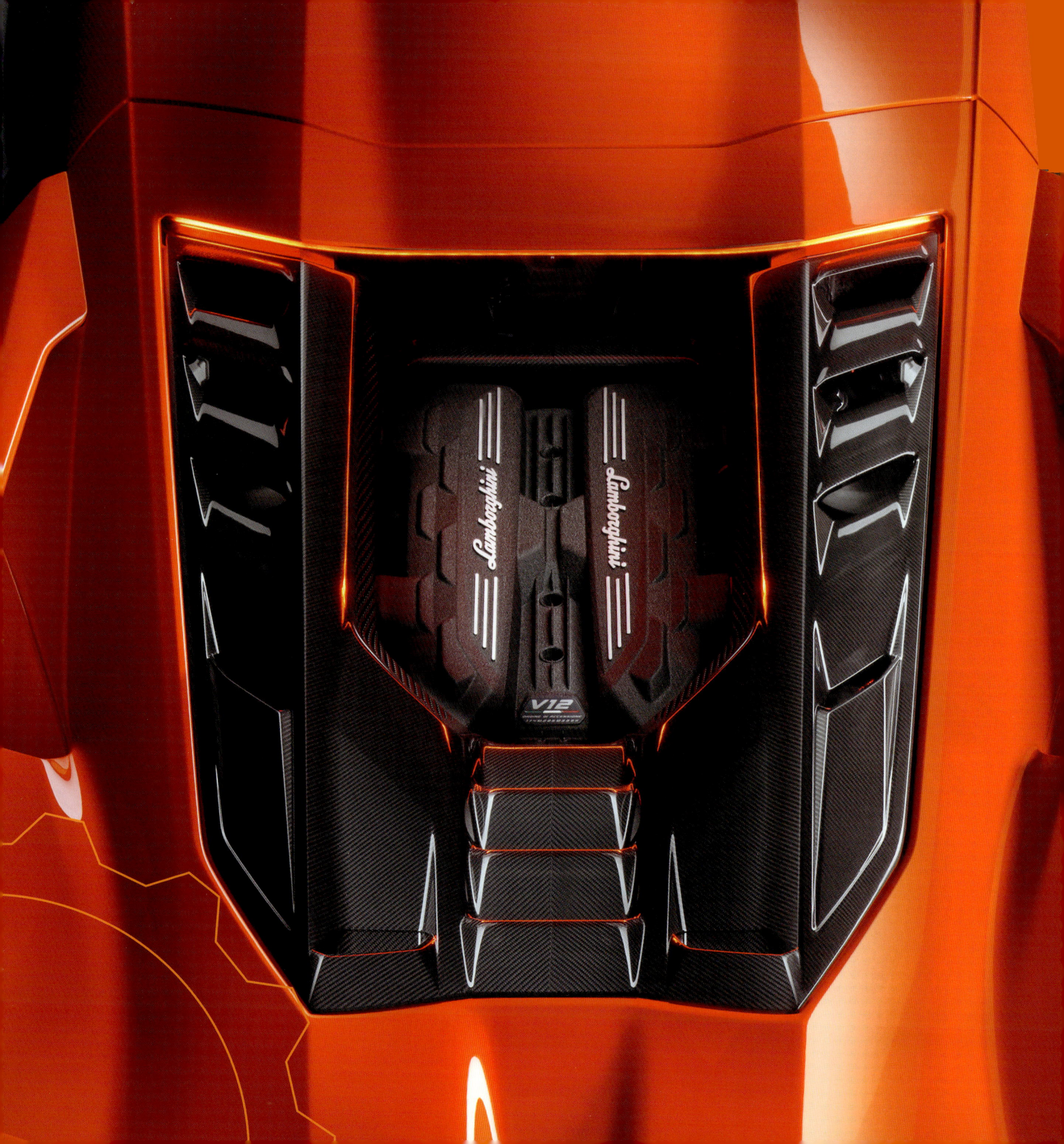

#9

WHY IT'S HERE
Lamborghini takes advantage of the latest technology to reimagine the driving experience, while preserving the naturally aspirated V12

LAMBORGHINI REVUELTO

"ALTHOUGH IT'S A HYBRID, THE REVUELTO'S V12 IS THE THING THAT TAKES CENTRE STAGE"

Air intake slash in the body side is functional but also distracts the eye from the Revuelto's longer wheelbase. But where would Lamborghini be without the scissor doors?

The Revuelto is the latest car in a bloodline that swirls all the way back to the Miura. Get past that car's almost ethereal beauty and it's worth remembering that Lamborghini has often been a disruptive tech leader, too. The Revuelto is, inevitably, a plug-in hybrid, but it's one that takes the possibilities of the format and does wild and wonderful things with it.

Lamborghini insists on the abbreviation HPEV to describe the new car, for 'high performance electrified vehicle'. This underlines that, while there are efficiencies here and a modest amount of pure electric running is available, really this is about exploring the dynamic and technical bandwidth of electrification. Performance is up by 30 per cent, emissions reduced by the same amount. These are impressive steps forward.

More than ever, the Revuelto is a Lamborghini that's dominated by its powertrain. This time we're talking naturally aspirated 6.5-litre V12, aided by three Yasa-supplied electric motors, two of which are mounted on the front axle, the third integrated into the new eight-speed dual-clutch transmission. For the first time, this sits behind the combustion engine and is positioned transversely. The central tunnel is where the gearbox used to live; now it's home to the 3.8 kWh lithium ion battery pack, that consists of 108, water-cooled pouch cells. The car can be plugged in and fully juiced up

Left and below, Y motif is a Lamborghini design signature that appears throughout the car

Right, Revuelto's nose cleverly incorporates two front cameras; they're modelled on missile launchers

in 30 minutes on a 7 KW power supply, or more likely replenished under regenerative braking. Are you ready for a Lambo trailing a power cable?

More on the combustion engine. It now makes 814bhp at 9,250rpm, and 535lb ft of torque. It's more powerful than the engine in the Aventador and can rev 1,000rpm higher. It's also been turned 180° in the engine bay compared to the old car, in order to accommodate the new gearbox, and at 218kg weighs 17kg less than before. The air intake ducts to the cylinders have been re-engineered to increase air flow to the combustion chamber, and there's a new crank and valvetrain. The compression ratio has been increased (12.6:1 now), and the exhaust has been reworked to reduce back-pressure at high revs.

Lamborghini reckons that four-wheel drive is one of its key attributes, although that hasn't always resulted in the sort of unadulterated driving dynamics you might expect from one of the world's most extrovert car makers. Hybridisation the Lambo way makes things seriously interesting on that front, though. The two electric motors on the front axle are oil-cooled axial flux units, chosen because they're more compact than a radial flux one and have a higher power and torque density. There's not a whole lot of space beneath the Revuelto's sharky nose, after all. Each motor produces 110 kW and weighs 18.5kg. Although they'll power the car when it's being driven purely in electric mode, their primary function is to improve performance and high speed dynamics via torque vectoring. Proper torque vectoring, that is, and not the sort

"THE REVUELTO HAS A TOTAL POWER OUTPUT OF 1001 BHP, ITS E-MOTOR BOOSTING THE 6.5-LITRE V12"

that relies on the brakes to function. Together with the third e-motor above the gearbox, the Revuelto is good for a total power output of 1,001bhp in maximum attack Corsa mode. Top speed is 217mph; zero to 62mph takes just 2.5 seconds. These are suitably punchy stats for the top Lamborghini.

Although this might be the most overtly digital car to have emerged from Sant'Agata, a vast amount of effort has gone into harmonising the constituent parts. To the extent that only one of them is allowed to take centre stage, and it's now louder than ever. "Everything started with the V12," Lamborghini's Chief Technical Officer Rouven Mohr explains. "We wanted a hybrid system that actually increases the perception of the V12. The mission was really to preserve the V12 identity. The hybrid is there to support you, to enable you to go faster, and most of all to improve the handling. You will not recognise that it's a hybrid. On the move, it feels like a much faster naturally aspirated V12, you're unaware of anything going on in the background. And it will feel like a car that's 150kg lighter because of the torque vectoring. It feels so agile and precise."

Consistency of response is another key precept. Mohr, it's worth noting, is a hip hop fan with a collection of historic Skyline GT-Rs at home. So although he has a super-computer for a brain, this is a man who savours the nuances of a car's dynamic behaviour and allows other, rather unexpected influences to filter through. Mohr insists that the Revuelto's complex new nervous system has been specifically calibrated to deliver greater bandwidth, more finesse than the Aventador, as good as it was, could manage.

The Revuelto's body uses active aero to deliver 66 per cent more downforce overall than its predecessor. There's a large front splitter and an extremely distinctive roof design that hustles the air flow to a pop-up rear wing. The old pushrod suspension has gone, liberating space at the front; there's a double wishbone multi-link set up front and rear, with magnetic dampers and clever control software. The new car uses a recalibrated version of Lamborghini's Dinamica Veicolo (LDVI) system; an army of accelerators and gyroscope sensors positioned at the car's centre of gravity provide real-time monitoring of lateral, longitudinal and vertical loads, as well as body roll, pitch and yaw, now also monitoring the torque vectoring. The front and rear anti-roll bars are stiffer, and Bridgestone has developed bespoke Potenza Sport rubber for the car. The brakes are new generation carbon ceramic, 410mm diameter at the front with 10 pistons, 390mm at the rear with four pistons. Of course, they have more to do now than ever. Under braking, the e-axle and rear e-motor contribute to the stopping process, allowing the friction brakes to recharge the battery more effectively. The Revuelto is a dizzying combination of hardware, software, and engineering instinct.

"At Nardo, we did more than 100 laps deciding when it was right to recuperate over the front axle, over the rear, and how much torque to use at the front," Mohr recalls. "This is where the magic happens. I don't know of any other hybrid that delivers this kind of performance and this sort of consistency. And that magic shouldn't be apparent to the driver. The hardware defines the boundary conditions of your playground, but I'd say 70 per cent is in the application. This really is a highly complex car,

The Revuelto has a completely reimagined interior. Main instrument display and central touchscreen have fantastic graphics. Good storage space, too

with so many parameters that can be influenced."

Drive modes now total 13: Recharge, Hybrid and Performance are new and can be mixed and matched, while Città mode is for silent running in city centres, with maximum power limited to 180bhp. Corsa mode, as ever, is the one that serves up the full 1000–plus bhp, the e-axle primed for maximum torque vectoring and all-wheel drive. There's an active rear axle, too, which we know from experience helps agility and high-speed stability.

Including its integrated e-motor, the DCT weighs 193kg; it's lighter, more space efficient and faster shifting than the system in the Huracan. A "continuous downshifting" feature allows it to cycle through multiple gears during downshifting, something the Aventador driver, who had his/her chiropractor on speed dial, could only dream of. The e-motor on the 'box acts as the starter motor and a generator, and also sends energy to the front axle. Depending on which drive mode is engaged, it acts independently of the gearbox and can help recharge the battery. Reverse gear is handled by the front e-motors, though the rear electric motor can get involved if you find yourself attempting a high-speed J-turn. Though we wouldn't really recommend it.

Especially as this thing is a riot of carbon fibre. Lamborghini refers to the Revuelto's new chassis as a "monofuselage", striving to exemplify the aeronautics connection. It's also about reducing weight wherever possible, to offset the extra kilos the e-motors and batteries incur, and improving structural rigidity. The new chassis is 10 per cent lighter than the Aventador's and, with a value of 40,000 Nm per degree, 25 per cent stiffer. The company's on site carbon fibre facility recently received a €65m investment and has been expanded; 340 people work there now. It takes 290 hours to manufacture the new monofuselage versus 170 for the old car. The

Revuelto uses forged carbon in its front crash cones, which are half the weight of the Aventador's aluminium impact structure, while delivering twice the energy absorption. The roof is made of pre-preg carbon fibre, labour intensively hand laid-up and laminated, vacuum-packed, then cooked in a huge autoclave. It's still the best process in terms of delivering the required aesthetic on your £400k hypercar.

Which brings us on to the Revuelto's design. All-new Lamborghinis are rare occurrences, but it does feel as though the company's Design Director Mitja Borkert has been teasing this one for a while now. The Terzio Millennio was his manifesto, and that dates back to the end of 2017. Then there was 2020's Sian, a more obvious precursor. The Revuelto expertly manages the extra 79mm it gains in its wheelbase, the black zig-zag element on the side there partly to distract the eye. Buttresses connect the roof to the rear wheelarches, an interlocking series of panels hustling air into the rear brakes and engine in an eye-poppingly geometric way. The Y-shaped front light motif is well established, the car's nose simpler, the twin front cameras cheekily modelled on missile launchers. Which leaves the rear to deliver most of the drama, from the complex diffuser to the high-mounted hexagonal exhaust, and most of all the open engine bay. Viewed from above, the Revuelto's rear three-quarters really are mesmerising.

"This is the result of the biggest design ideation ever done at Lamborghini," Borkert explains. "We did more than 17 third scale models. All the lines on the car are embracing the monocoque, they're embracing the engine. There is never a definite starting point, but the research began as soon as I arrived at Lamborghini [in 2016]. The engineering, ergonomics and aero package are all rigorously defined and then you find the sweet spot in terms of the proportions and the wheelbase. We all influence each other, although on a car that has the sort of performance that this one has, every single surface on the body will obviously be doing something."

He continues, "There's more space inside but it's only 2.5cm taller than the Aventador. A lot of focus was placed on the entry into the car, on the drama of getting in. The doors open six degrees further out now."

Borkert likens the open and visible engine to the sort of thing you see on a superbike, and says that it was an approach the late Ferdinand Piëch (who masterminded VW's purchase of Lamborghini back in 1998) appreciated when he had an early preview. "He always said that designers never cared about the engine, so he really liked this. We're really celebrating it."

The cockpit is superb. A new steering wheel with a thinner rim groups the "drive mode" button on the top left of the spar, with an EV button on the right. They're little anodised switches and they feel great under your thumb. Ahead lies the configurable instrument screen, housed in a slender binnacle. The graphics are fabulous. An air vent that resembles an angry space invader sits at the top of the central display, which floats above a usefully sized storage space. At last, somewhere to put your phone. Screen content can be swiped across to a display for the passenger. The hazard warning light and fuel tank button live in little bezels. There are 360 degree cameras to ease the perennial embarrassment of reverse-parking a big mid-engined Italian hypercar. It all feels high quality and highly tactile, a more recent and very welcome Lamborghini USP.

And the name? Revuelto was a fighting bull, a celebrity in the arenas of Barcelona in the 1880s, who made numerous bids for freedom. By all accounts, he was quite a character, but the closest English translation is "mixed up". "We thought it was a good way of explaining how we've blended the two souls of this car," Stephan Winkelmann explains. "We will always be better in terms of performance than the generation before, but we will also be more sustainable. If we want to continue to be a super sports car manufacturer, we have to adapt, we have to find solutions."

Wise words, but the proof is in the driving. Time to find out…

SPECIFICATION

ENGINE
Revuelto uses a naturally aspirated 6.5-litre V12 aided by three e-motors fed by a 3.8kWh battery

CHASSIS
Carbon fibre is used extensively in Revuelto's body to reduce weight and improve rigidity

GEARBOX
Eight-speed dual-clutch transmission is mounted transversely behind engine

AERO
Revuelto uses active aero to deliver 66 per cent more downforce than the Aventador

VEHICLE TYPE –
Mid-engined, rear-wheel drive coupe

POWERTRAIN –
Naturally aspirated 6.5-litre V12, 814bhp plus e-motor (187bhp), for a total power output of 1001bhp, 534lb ft @6,750rpm, 3.8 kWh lithium ion battery

WEIGHT: 1,772kg (dry)

DIMENSIONS –
LENGTH: 4,947mm
WIDTH: 2,266mm
HEIGHT: 1,160mm

TRANSMISSION –
Eight-speed dual clutch

PERFORMANCE –
Top speed 217mph
0–62mph 2.5 seconds

161
BRAIN-FRAZZLING FACT:

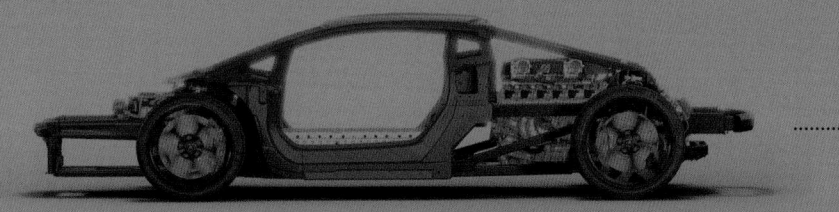

THE REVUELTO HAS A DRIFT MODE ALTHOUGH LAMBORGHINI DOESN'T ACTUALLY CALL IT THAT. "GO INTO SPORT MODE AND THERE'S A MORE REAR-DRIVE BIAS AND A GREATER SLIP ANGLE," SAYS THE COMPANY'S CHIEF TECHNICAL OFFICER, ROUVEN MOHR. "OR IF YOU WANT MORE OF A FOUR-WHEEL SLIDE GO TO ESC CORSA OFF. SO YES, YOU CAN DRIFT IT. THE BOUNDARIES OF THIS CAR REALLY ARE ON ANOTHER LEVEL."

DRIVING THE REVUELTO

Lamborghini has often felt like the last dinosaur, roaring forlornly in the face of electric's meteoric impact. No more. The Revuelto is a revolutionary Raging Bull. The replacement for the Aventador, Lamborghini's biggest beast, is now a plug-in hybrid. It features three electric motors, there is no reverse gear, that's done electrically. There's no clumsiness either – the handling is far more sophisticated, so too the electrical integration. The gearbox no longer thrashes your head back and forth like a heavy metaller in a mosh pit. There's more space in the cabin and – hallelujah – the seats are no longer as pious as a church pew, but instead embrace and coddle.

The technical make-up is nothing particularly new, though. With an e-motor for each front wheel, plus another between engine and gearbox, drawing power from a slimline battery tucked down behind the seats, it puts the same pieces in the same places as the Porsche 918 Spider did a decade ago. A template copied by everything from the Honda NSX to the Revuelto's closest rival from down the Po valley, Ferrari's SF90.

But this one has a V12. Where others have downsized, fitted turbocharged V6s or V8s, they've kept the power, but arguably lost a little charisma. Not the Revuelto. Yes you can drive it around on pure electric power, but only for about 6–8 miles because the battery is a piddling 3.8kWh. That's because electric is the support act, the V12 remaining the star of the show.

The 6.5-litre nat-asp engine is the lightest, most powerful 12 cylinder ever made by Lamborghini. It's been rotated through 180°, putting the gearbox out the back rather than in front (as that's where the battery now sits). Rather than the ISR single shaft gearbox that felt old even when the Aventador arrived back in 2011, there is a brand new eight-speed twin clutch system, connected to the rear wheels. The fronts are driven by electricity. And algorithms.

The Revuelto's fiery combustion heart develops 814bhp. Electricity thickens this up to 1001bhp, yielding 0–62mph in 2.5secs and a top speed beyond 218mph. It's deeply fast, sounds sublime and uses its 187bhp of electric power subtly. But what it also does is provide instant initial thrust out of corners while the internal combustion instrument is still tuning up.

Coming out of a slow corner you feel the electric motors work the front wheels to negate understeer and keep the line tight. But it's not blunt force, it's nuanced, the power evenly and effectively distributed between the wheels. This is what's new and interesting about the Revuelto. The Aventador didn't have brilliant chassis finesse, its 4WD system was comparatively crude, but its replacement, despite the considerable extra complexity, is way more fluent and sophisticated to drive. It involves you more in the process, and as a result, rewards more. It's not all about the engine, well, not until you're pointing straight and the revs have started to climb beyond 5,000 on their way to a suitably roaring, operatic 9,500rpm crescendo.

Steering feel is good, although information comes as much through your back side as the wheel rim. What's changed is the overall sense of balance and pliancy. The Aventador was a handful on the limit, whereas this feels more controlled and capable. In fact, this is the closest Lamborghini has yet come to challenging Ferrari's world-class chassis dynamics. The Revuelto is not only deeply dramatic and exciting to drive, but this new level of control and integration adds real depth to the experience.

The chassis supports semi-active suspension, and braking is carbon ceramic with 10 piston front calipers grabbing 410mm discs. Plus there's regenerative braking on top. Integrating friction and electric braking has tripped up almost every car maker. We couldn't spot the handover here. It never feels less than natural – with the small caveat that our first drive happens on a track, so we're using the brakes hard. They're too sharp at the top of their travel, but otherwise feel reassuring and easily capable of dealing with a kerbweight that has gone up over 200kg from the Aventador. The 1,772kg figure is a dry weight, so you're looking at over 1,900kg with fluids.

The gearbox fires the shifts through with zero fuss and where the Aventador was pretty wooden and unyielding, the Revuelto is feelsome and full-blooded. There's a little body roll. Not much, but enough to feel

"THE REVUELTO'S HYPERCAR RIVALS HAVE DOWNSIZED THEIR ENGINES. BUT THIS ONE IS A V12"

cushioning as well as support, a sense it's not just rigidly controlled despite the fact it wears giant 355-width back tyres on 22-inch rims and features anti-roll bars that are now 11 per cent stiffer at the front and 50 per cent at the back. The ride has some give in it, while unwanted noise and vibration seem better filtered. This hypercar might be the most red-blooded of all, but it has genuine bandwidth.

And more practicality, too. Unlike the Ferrari SF90, there's a proper boot in the nose, while the packaging efforts inside have resulted in 84mm additional cabin length, an extra 25mm headroom, and notably more elbow space. Over your shoulder there's now room for a golf bag. And there's thoughtfully considered storage space for your phone. And also a cupholder.

It's still very much a Lamborghini, with a windscreen that stretches away to a virtual infinity point, and a low header rail. But this feels brighter and easier to see out of than before (apart from out the back), as if the designers and engineers have considered the ergonomics properly. Even the steering wheel, in fact. It looks overloaded, but actually it's logically laid out. The upper knobs on each side control the powertrain, drive modes on the left (City, Strada, Sport, Corsa) and EV settings (Recharge, Hybrid and Performance) on the right. Combine them and there are 13 different dynamic settings to choose from. The lower left controls the dampers (and nose lift) and the lower right does the aero.

Yes, aerodynamics. The headline figures here are a 61 per cent improvement in drag efficiency over the Aventador and 66 per cent more downforce. The former is more important than the latter. This is not a track warrior à la GT3 RS, but a broader based feelgood hypercar.

Retaining the V12 is a major USP, and also means the Revuelto has kept the character and charisma that makes Lamborghinis such a force of nature to drive. The added layer of polish and dynamism? That's entirely new and more than welcome. It also shines a light down the path for other Lamborghinis to follow, as well as proving that charisma doesn't have to be dimmed by hybridisation. Way to go, Lambo.

The Revuelto's outrageous shape is something of a support structure for the 6.5-litre V12 engine, which is visible in the centre of the car

10

WHY IT'S HERE
The grand masters of lightweight sports car engineering enter the fully electric fray in serious style. It's a Lotus like none before

LOTUS EVIJA

The Evija's interior adds a new dimension of purposeful luxury to the company's usually rather minimal proposition. Though you'll be too busy holding on to appreciate the tactility of the materials

I t's said that in the moments before your brain decides you're going to check out, time puts the brakes on. Fractions of a second melt into minutes, creating enough space to contemplate the futility of existence and fully observe the unpleasantness that's unfolding. Well, it's true, because we've just gone full *Matrix*.

It started with a fizz, the unmistakeable sound of rear tyres spinning up, has progressed to an angle not entirely parallel with the straight piece of track we're supposed to be launching down, and now we're heading directly, and at some speed, for a large puddle on which we will almost certainly aquaplane before the final, full interface with the Norfolk Broads.

Turns out that the brain is a total drama queen, because somehow the car rights itself and we're soon pointing in the right direction once again. In hindsight, performing a standing launch on a wet track in a 1,600bhp passive prototype – no active aero, no traction control, no ESC, no torque-vectoring, basic ABS – on Trofeo R tyres probably wasn't the best idea, but that's the thing about the Lotus Evija, its unfathomable performance is so accessible and exploitable that it lulls you into a false sense of security.

A big off is never ideal, but especially not today as we're at Lotus' famed Hethel test track, about to become the first outsiders in the world to experience the Evija from behind the wheel. Half the workforce is watching from the pit wall, including the boss Matt Windle. It's an honour but also a big responsibility, and the Evija's raw numbers weigh heavily on the mind. In finished form the 130 examples will cost £2.4m each. For that you get four motors, four-wheel drive, 1,972bhp, 0–62mph in well under three seconds, 0–124mph in six seconds, and perhaps most startling of all it'll go from 124mph to 186mph in half the time it takes a Bugatti Chiron. For today's exercise we've only got access to 1,600bhp, 1250lb ft of torque and a top speed capped at 140mph… But we're pretty sure we'll manage.

This isn't just a halo car for Lotus, it's a flagbearer for really fast electric cars as a whole. If Lotus can make this one stick, then the supercar's future is all but secure. It'll also get the next phase of Lotus' rejuvenation under the Geely umbrella off to the best possible start, and Windle's plans are punchy: the combustion-engined, Evija-inspired Emira is up and running, the hugely impressive Eletre is rapidly establishing itself, and there's more to come. Beyond Emira, which will stick around "into the late Twenties," says

169

Windle, Lotus will become a pure-electric car maker. The Evija isn't just a one-off here to demonstrate Lotus technical ability, then, it's a signpost for the entire future of the company.

Speak to the people behind the project and it's clear they're well aware of the traditional electric car limitations – range, weight, emotion – but for every hurdle, they see an engineering opportunity and Lotus was never going to blindly follow the pack. Unlike the flat skateboard battery you'll find in most mainstream EVs these days, or even the T-shaped pack in the Rimac Nevera and Pininfarina Battista, all the cells sit behind you in a dramatic pyramid-shaped pile. "We wanted the cockpit-forward feel of a classic Group C racer," says Gavin Kershaw, the man responsible for making all Lotuses handle like Lotuses. "Plus you couldn't sit this low, and the roof would have been 200mm higher."

Engineers settled on a 93kWh battery – bigger than the 69kWh first mooted but still some way behind the Rimac's 120kWh pack and way, way behind the 200kWh slab Elon wants to put in the eternally gestating Tesla Roadster. But then this is a Lotus so there had to be a trade-off between being the lightest car in its class (1,887kg in its most featherweight spec), delivering a useable WLTP range of 250 miles, and making sure you can get some decent lap time in. Kershaw reckons the Evija is good for about 15 laps or 30 miles flat out, before it's time for a charge. "Don't forget this is a car that can do 0–186mph in less than nine seconds and accelerate at over 1g for all of that, so you'd need to be an F1 driver to cope with any more track time," he points out.

Even when it's stationary, it's lightning fast: "We can charge up to 500kW, although it's not readily available at the moment," says Louis Kerr, Evija Chief Platform Engineer. "We can do 350kW easily, that takes about 12 mins. With 500kW we'll do it in sub nine minutes, for a full charge." The cooling is purposefully overkill, too, and an area that is often overlooked on electric cars. "We have a lot of radiators, so we're over-cooled in road conditions. You can push it on track and won't have any loss in power."

What you feel right away is that low centre of gravity, officially lower than an Emira, but unlike a skateboard chassis with the mass spread out towards all four corners, the Evija really wants to rotate, to change direction on a pin head – a big benefit of concentrating all that mass in the middle of the car. "We liken it to someone in an office chair. Put their arms and legs out and try to rotate them, it takes a lot of effort," Kershaw explains. "Get them to curl up into a ball and you can flick them from side-to-side."

Could an electric car ever feel truly like a Lotus? Yes, is the answer, as surprising as it seems. It's there, from the first corner, the DNA. Make no mistake, it's crude in here, there's no trim whatsoever, just a mass of wires and metal, but that's helping concentrate the mind on what's important. The steering is superb, light and darty around the dead-ahead, then loading up according to wheel angle and speed. The brakes, Brembo's top-shelf carbon-ceramics, baked to perfection for no less than nine months, really deliver the goods, too. There's loads of feel, they're easy to modulate, and have enough bite to shed the silly numbers that are being so effortlessly accrued. For the less aggressive driving modes (there will be five, on a manettino-style dial on the steering wheel – Range, City, Tour, Sport and Track), most retardation will be regen, bleeding into physical friction when you need it. On track you'll be in full control of pad on disc.

But it's the way this thing moves that's just staggering. There's so much less inertia than you thought there would be, it doesn't feel cumbersome, it's light on its feet, playful and with the instant smash of acceleration even a naturally aspirated engine could only fantasise about. You have to keep reminding yourself this is far from finished because the handling balance is already so polished. There's a little body roll, which is welcome, but also a satisfying balance in the chassis, like it's working all four tyres evenly.

There's joy in simply controlling and managing the mass, feeling your way around the track; it's miles from the point and squirt device we'd assumed it would be. And there's still ESC, trick traction control with a hero sideways mode, four-wheel torque vectoring… and another 400bhp

Opposite, as with the exterior, the Evija's cockpit plays with the idea of 'porosity'. There are lots of open spaces

"THE EVIJA REALLY WANTS TO ROTATE AND CHANGE DIRECTION LIKE A TRUE LOTUS. IT FEELS AGILE"

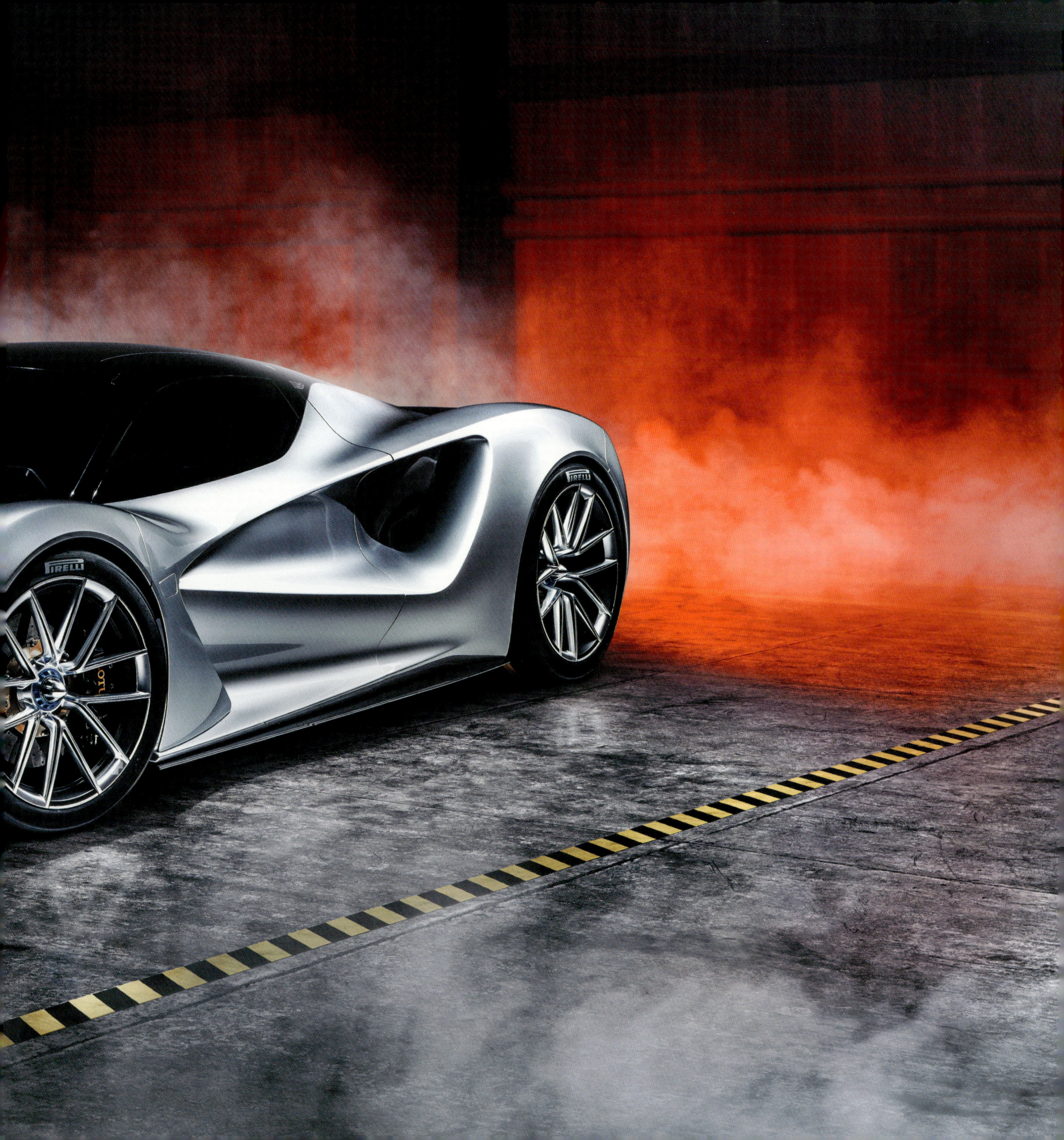

(400bhp!) to come. Right now, the torque split is locked at 25 per cent front, 75 rear, which would explain its penchant for oversteer if you tickle the throttle a hair early in the corners, but mainly it just grips and rips, despite fairly modest 265-width front tyres. It really is quite something.

Pin it from standing in the dry (no need for clever software, just mash the throttle, an idiot could do it) and it's not so much the initial force that surprises you – Teslas and Taycans and lots of other BEVs have conditioned us to that now – but the way that, with no gearchanges, it just keeps coming, a huge wall of unrelenting shove. In fact, it actually ramps up, accelerating harder the faster you go, feeding in the hit of the whole fruit as and when the tyres can handle it until you're staring wide-eyed at some enormous number on the dash in front of you and wondering how on earth you got there.

And it's all so easy. Even a twin-clutch gearbox requires some management, some knowledge of when to shift, at what rpm the engine comes off the boil, but this is just a two-pedal go-kart, albeit one with a sizeable rocket up its bum. The noise? A shrill wail that intensifies exponentially – a good fit for the driving experience to be fair – that'll be dampened down once the guys fit some sound deadening, and pump something synthetic through the speakers and add an actual interior. We're confident.

We're shown around a next-stage prototype,

There have been a lot of striking looking cars in Lotus's long history, but the £2.4m Evija might be the best of the lot

"THE EVIJA ISN'T JUST A HALO CAR FOR LOTUS, IT'S A FLAGBEARER FOR FAST ELECTRIC CARS AS A WHOLE"

SPECIFICATION

CHASSIS
Single piece carbon fibre monocoque helps off-set weight penalty incurred by big battery pack

POWERTRAIN
Rather than a skateboard configuration, the batteries are arranged in a pyramid behind the cockpit

DESIGN
Body features lots of open space, including a venturi tunnel through each rear three-quarter

AERO
Bi-plane front splitter's central area provides air to cool battery, outer sections cool the e-axle

VEHICLE TYPE –
Fully electric, all-wheel drive coupe

POWERTRAIN –
Four electric motors, 93kWh battery, 1,972bhp, 1,284lb ft with torque vectoring

WEIGHT: 1,887kg

DIMENSIONS –
Length: 4,459mm
Width: 2,000mm
Height: 1,122mm

TRANSMISSION –
Four single-speed planetary

PERFORMANCE –
Top speed 217mph 0–62mph in 2.8 seconds
0–186mph in less than nine seconds

BRAIN-FRAZZLING FACT:

THE LOTUS EVIJA CAN ACCELERATE FROM 0-186MPH IN UNDER NINE SECONDS, AND PULL 1G FOR THAT LENGTH OF TIME. A DRIVER WOULD NEED TO HAVE FORMULA ONE LEVELS OF FITNESS TO COPE WITH THAT SORT OF PHYSICAL FORCE ON A REPEATED BASIS. DESPITE THE CAR'S HI-TECH SPEC, IT USES AN OLD-SCHOOL ELECTRO-HYDRAULIC STEERING SYSTEM FOR THE MAXIMUM AMOUNT OF DRIVER COMMUNICATION.

The Evija is a triumph of design and packaging. Those rear intakes allow a clear view through and down the side of the car

stripped down and up on jacks in Factory Three, the building where Evijas will be bolted together, the same building the VX220 and Lotus Carlton were built in. We take our chance to marvel at the components on show, the finest money can buy. There's a two motor, two inverter assembly that would fit in a gym bag – that's 1,000bhp right there. A 12kg disc – one for each wheel – and the 6:1 single speed gearbox. There is also a third F1-style heave damper, to keep the car level under extreme downforce. Finally, one of the world's largest, single-piece carbon-fibre tubs with built in sub frames for maximum stiffness. The list goes on and not much is missing, as far as we can tell.

And we haven't even mentioned the way this thing looks yet. The basic shape is breathtaking. It's a harmony of soft, flowing curves and holes, rather than angles and aero add-ons, and proof that you can adhere to classic mid-engined proportions and still produce something titillating and different. Some people have likened it to a Barbara Hepworth sculpture, but the porosity is good for aero and cooling.

Whatever preconceptions you might still have about an electric Lotus, the Evija simply obliterates them. Once you've ridden the lightning, you will want more. In fact, you'll want all you can get. What an amazing car.

"FOR EVERY OBSTACLE THEY FACE, THE LOTUS GUYS SEE AN ENGINEERING OPPORTUNITY"

 **#11**

WHY IT'S HERE
Because creating a hypercar is about pushing things to the extreme. And the Speedtail is *extreme*

MCLAREN SPEEDTAIL

"CLIMB INTO THE CENTRE SEAT, LOOK ABOVE YOU, AND YOU'LL SEE A BUTTON MARKED 'VELOCITY'"

"WHAT'S ADMIRABLE IS THE WAY THE INTAKES AND AIR CHANNELS HAVE BEEN HIDDEN AWAY"

Sleek, isn't it? Long and low and lean and, well, sleek. A streamliner. A car from the future in the here and now. This is it, the McLaren Speedtail, the machine formerly known as BP23 and likely forever known as the spiritual successor to the F1. Three seats, stratospheric top speed and a price tag that's similarly out of this world.

The McLaren Speedtail cost each of its 106 owners north of £2.1m for a car that boasts 1,036bhp and a 250mph maximum speed. When they strap themselves into the centre seat, line up on a runway, press the Velocity button above their head and nail the throttle, they'll feel what it's like to accelerate from zero to 186mph in the same time it takes a diesel supermini to hit 60mph. McLaren likes its Ultimate Series cars to answer questions. Take the Senna, which answers, "Is it possible to road-legalise racing levels of downforce?" Turns out it is, and few cars come close to the 800kg of downward pressure the Senna is able to produce at 150mph, with hugely thrilling results. Now we're in the realm of, "What if we forgot about downforce and went low-drag instead? Say grand touring was still a thing, what would the ultimate 21st-century GT car look like? What would it be able to do?"

McLaren's leap of faith is that grand touring is still a thing, and that people will want to do it as a threesome. Hyper GT is the pitch, Bugatti Chiron, even if McLaren isn't admitting as much, the target. The Speedtail is about luxury as much as it is speed. Well, heading that way. We'll come on to talk about the clean lines of the cabin, the tactility of the materials, but first just look at it: the length of the tail, the elegance of those rear lines. It's plain stunning, a shape that treats the air passing over and around it with respect. Nothing on the road looks quite like the Speedtail.

What air it needs is subtly taken, used as appropriate for combustion or cooling and then calmly reintroduced, before being precisely and delicately detached by the samurai blade tail. At 5.13 metres long, it's 60cm longer than a Chiron, the sweeping carbon cape carrying with it a suggestion of art deco/steampunk Thirties cool. A Rocketeer kind of car. That's the back, at least. The front is more challenging. What initially springs to mind are mid-Eighties concept cars, stuff such as the MG EX-E and the Lotus Etna. Cool, if unlikely, reference points, and something to do with the wheelspats and low, low nose. The more you look, the better it gets, though, and it's admirable how the intakes and air channels have been hidden away.

Still, at this end of the car, engineering is more important than aesthetics. McLaren's design boss describes it as a "comet, with the mass at the front, then this long tail." Though they look a little odd, the Speedtail would not have been able to deliver on its top speed and acceleration parameters without its spats. They remain static as the wheel rotates and reduce turbulence almost entirely, the air allowed only to escape from the wheelarch through a single notch, smoothing flow. They can be removed, but McLaren suggests you don't. Just think of the brake dust

The McLaren Speedtail is an engineering and aesthetic challenge. Think comet, with the mass at the front followed by a long, long tail build-up. And did you notice? No exterior mirrors. Instead, pop-out cameras with screens at the base of the A-pillars. The transition from window into roofline is artfully done – there's no header rail, nothing to delay the air's passage. And how about the cuts at the back of the rear deck? This area is made of flexible carbon fibre, moved by hydraulic actuators to adjust the centre of pressure or aid braking stability. We must assume that somewhere in Woking that vast one-piece clamshell must have been air- but also child-proofed, being continuously flexed, bent and pressurised so that the Speedtail can resist the challenges of Casino Square.

Which, let's face it, is a likely destination. Let's just hope it's been able to use a decent proportion of that 1,036bhp on the way. The balance between combustion engine and e-motor(s) works out as 731bhp from the familiar 4.0-litre twin turbo V8 and 305bhp of electric. There's a conventional battery pack, but no plug-in socket. It uses inductive charging instead.

Don't get too hung up on the stats. Only 7mph faster than the 25-year old F1, a mere 1,036bhp total when Koenigsegg's Agera RS has a full megawatt (1,341bhp), and the Chiron has 1,479bhp. And 1,650bhp seems the entry point if you want to talk 300mph. But perhaps that's the point. McLaren isn't talking 300mph, because the faster you want to go, the more you have to compromise; stiffer tyre sidewalls are just the beginning. Going back to first principles, McLaren wants the Speedtail to answer the hyper-GT question, not simply battle for bigger numbers. Seen from that point of view, it's hard to conclude that 250mph isn't ludicrously adequate. So 250mph it is, reached very quickly. Really, who could possibly grumble about 250mph?

We can also assume McLaren is focusing on high-speed stability as a core facet, to make distance relaxing and undemanding. Wind and tyre noise need to be minimised – in that respect, it's encouraging that the front tyres are modest 235-section, that there's nothing to snag the air passing over the canopy. Its fuel tank can carry 72 litres. Comparing and contrasting the Speedtail is all well and good, but its USP isn't speed, but seating. A central seat is captivating, almost instantly a more logical, sensible place to sit in the car, distanced from both A-pillars, the symmetry of the view out an utter joy. The catch is getting in. Various techniques are available; none is elegant. Or quick. McLaren has incorporated recessed handles in the headlining, and engineered "directional leather" that aids sliding in, then "subtly holds the occupant in place while they drive." This was necessary because the central seat couldn't have high bolsters. You do miss them.

If you want to feel wedged in, drop back into one of the flanking chairs. Here, tucked behind B-pillar, shoulder overlapped with the driver, you are genuinely hemmed in. It's comfortable but restrictive. You can't be big. The view out, however, is, like the driver's, unique. It's a special place to sit, and you're aware of views in interesting directions, of the amount of light, of angles you've never seen before in a car.

The centre seat makes the Speedtail egocentric. The symmetry is emphasised by how much it's been decluttered. No sun visors; instead, the Speedtail is fitted with electrochromic glass, which darkens at the press of a button. The LED interior lights have been incorporated into the glass, too. Your eye has less to fall on, and the clean view across the swathe of screen and air vent, mirrored either side, channels you into focusing on the steering wheel, finished in this glorious wood-like machined carbon. That material, super-tactile, carved from billet carbon where each layer is just 30 microns thick, is used for the paddles too, and forms the binnacle around the porthole above your head. That's where you find the car controls, buttons for gearlever, start/stop and switchable dynamic modes.

The most interesting one is labelled Velocity. This prepares the Speedtail for high speeds. "No extra key or anything," design lead Andy Palmer explains, "this will do 250mph straight out of the box." It lowers, the active aero is optimised and the wing cameras fold away. Whether this makes it an illegal mode on the road, like the P1's Track mode, McLaren has yet to admit. The doors operate electrically, there are stowage drawers underneath the outer seats, load bays at either end (162 litres in total, fitted luggage

> **"THE SPEEDTAIL IS A HYPER-GT, AND A 250MPH TOP SPEED IS THEREFORE MORE THAN ADEQUATE"**

Right, door handles retract to create a seamless body of remarkable aerodynamism

Everything about the Speedtail is engineered to perfection. It's a hyper-GT, so that includes the audio system

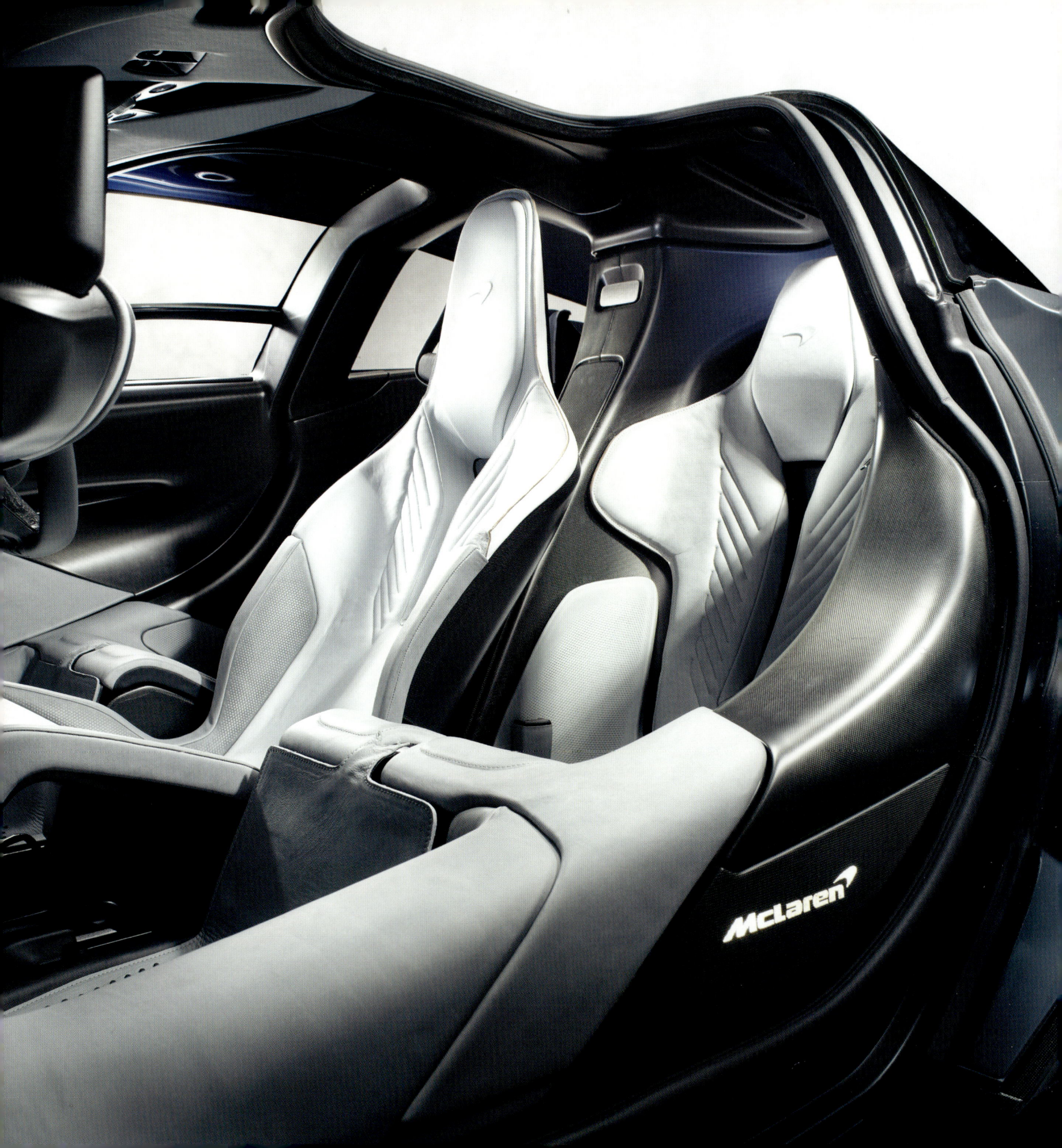

matched to the interior specification is optional) but no lockers in the flanks à la F1... more's the pity. Cupholders? Those are on the options list.

But it's not just the tech and layout that separates the Speedtail from lesser McLarens – it's the design and quality. So here we have Scandinavian leather where air is infused beneath the surface during manufacturing, to reduce density and cut weight by 30 per cent. It's still sufficiently tough that, with stippling to aid grip, McLaren has used it in place of carpet on the floor. Then there's Titanium Deposition Carbon Fibre (McLaren does love a scientific sounding name). Carbo-tanium gets around the issue of coloured carbon fibre, which can, apparently, compromise the material's structural integrity. Here, a micron-thin titanium layer is fused onto the carbon weave. McLaren has left the finish natural on this Speedtail, but the titanium can be anodised in any colour – you could even have images and words placed into the carbon. What's the betting that some owners have gone this route?

McLaren pioneered carbon fibre. Now it's taking it to the next level. Does the rest of the car do the same thing for the driving experience?

DRIVING THE SPEEDTAIL

Why does placing the steering wheel and the driver's seat in the centre of a car's cabin make it feel so special? Why does it tug at the emotional connection between man and machine so much more than it really should? The moment you pop open the McLaren Speedtail's dihedral door and shuffle over a passenger seat squab into the slender, solo bucket seat, the huge price becomes irrelevant.

Increasingly, the static drama super and hypercars can generate is the currency on which they trade – the opportunities to use any of their full potential are just too infrequent. As-quoted performance has become less important, the need to dazzle with bizarre styling and violent,

aggressive shapes has set in and, gradually, the hypercar has transformed from being an object of beauty to a collection of jarring angles.

The McLaren Speedtail is the antidote to the aesthetic of extremism. It is pure elegance and delicacy – smooth aerodynamic forms and deportment. How ironic that this shape – futuristic but clearly referencing beautiful forms from the past – should have come from the same place that gave us the visual headbutt that is the Senna. You will either love the way McLaren has perched a few added feet of carbon fibre onto the rump of a 720S, or hate it – but you can probably guess that we think it's remarkably wonderful. And it is, in the finest tradition of car styling, primarily influenced by the intended activity of the vehicle itself – in this case, very high speeds. The Speedtail has a claimed top speed of 250mph. Having driven a Chiron and felt the way the McLaren pulls north of 200, we'd venture that that claim seems very conservative. Until now, the real speed kings have bullied their way into the serious 200s through brute motive force, but this car slips through the air with the type of disconcerting lack of drag that marks it out as something truly different. Something more akin to an old-school endurance racing car.

Still, big numbers require big numbers, and this car has 1,036bhp from a hybridised 4.0-litre twin-turbocharged V8, feeding a dual-clutch gearbox, pounding into the road surface through only the rear tyres. Minnow stats compared with a Chiron, but the Brit counters with a bantam 1,430kg kerbweight which leaves its power-to-weight figure much closer to the Big Bug than you might imagine. And, boy, does it deliver something worthy of those figures.

A damp airfield isn't the ideal venue for a first meeting but we rise to the occasion nonetheless. With the traction control set to Track mode for the lightest hand of intervention, the Speedtail is

The Speedtail's wheel spats may be controversial as design devices but they're functional: they remain static as the wheel rotates to reduce turbulence

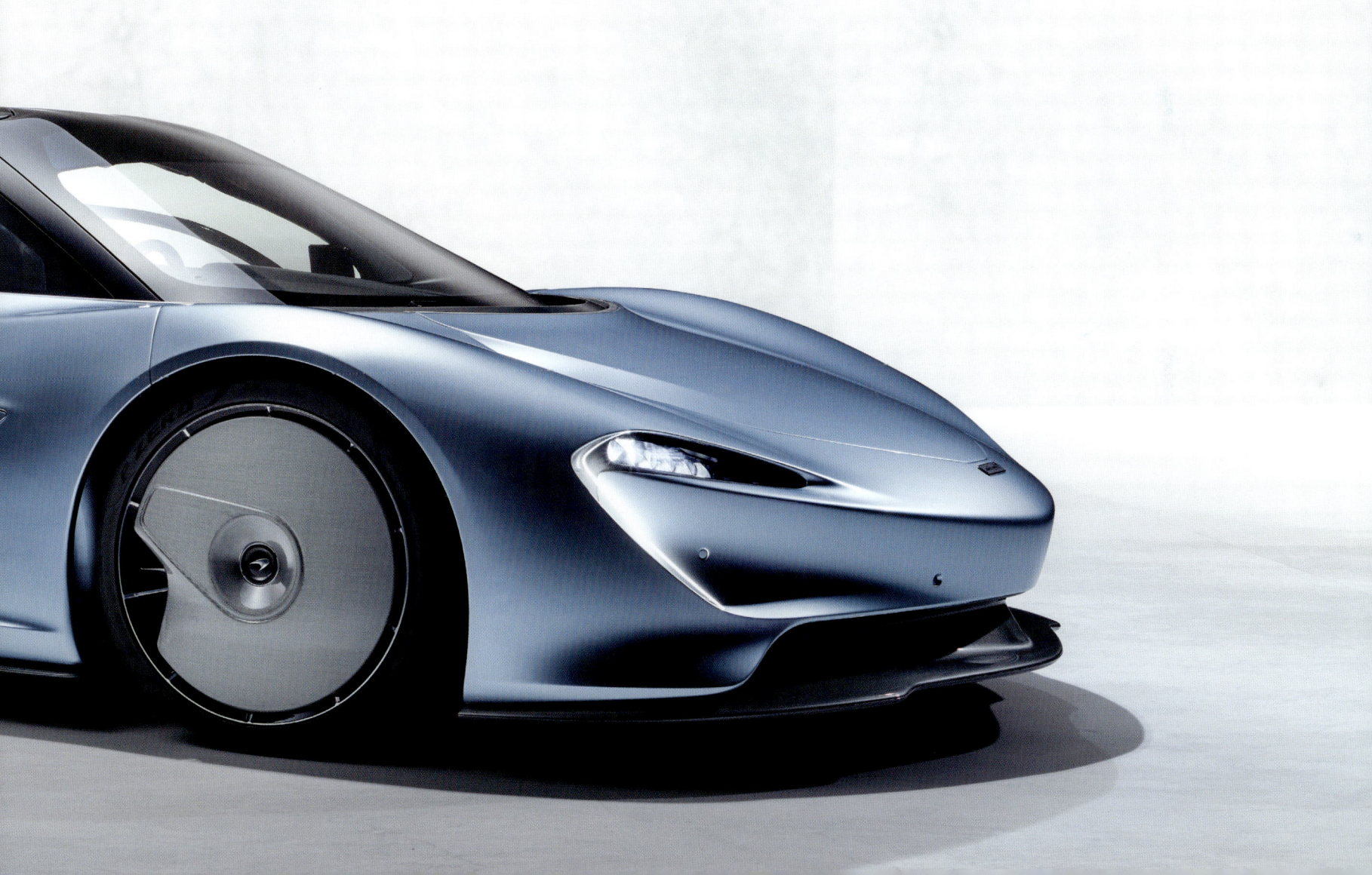

SPECIFICATION

AERO
SPEEDTAIL IS VERY AERO-DRIVEN. VELOCITY MODE LOWERS THE CAR, AND PRIMES THE ACTIVE AERO

BODY
BIG DIHEDRAL DOORS OPEN WIDE TO ADMIT THREE PASSENGERS, WITH DRIVER IN THE MIDDLE

POWERTRAIN
4.0-LITRE TWIN TURBO V8 MAKES 731BHP AIDED HERE BY A 308BHP E-MOTOR. HELL OF A HYBRID

DETAILS
WHEEL SPATS AREN'T VERY PRETTY BUT THEY TIDY UP THE DIRTY AIR AROUND THE FRONT ARCHES

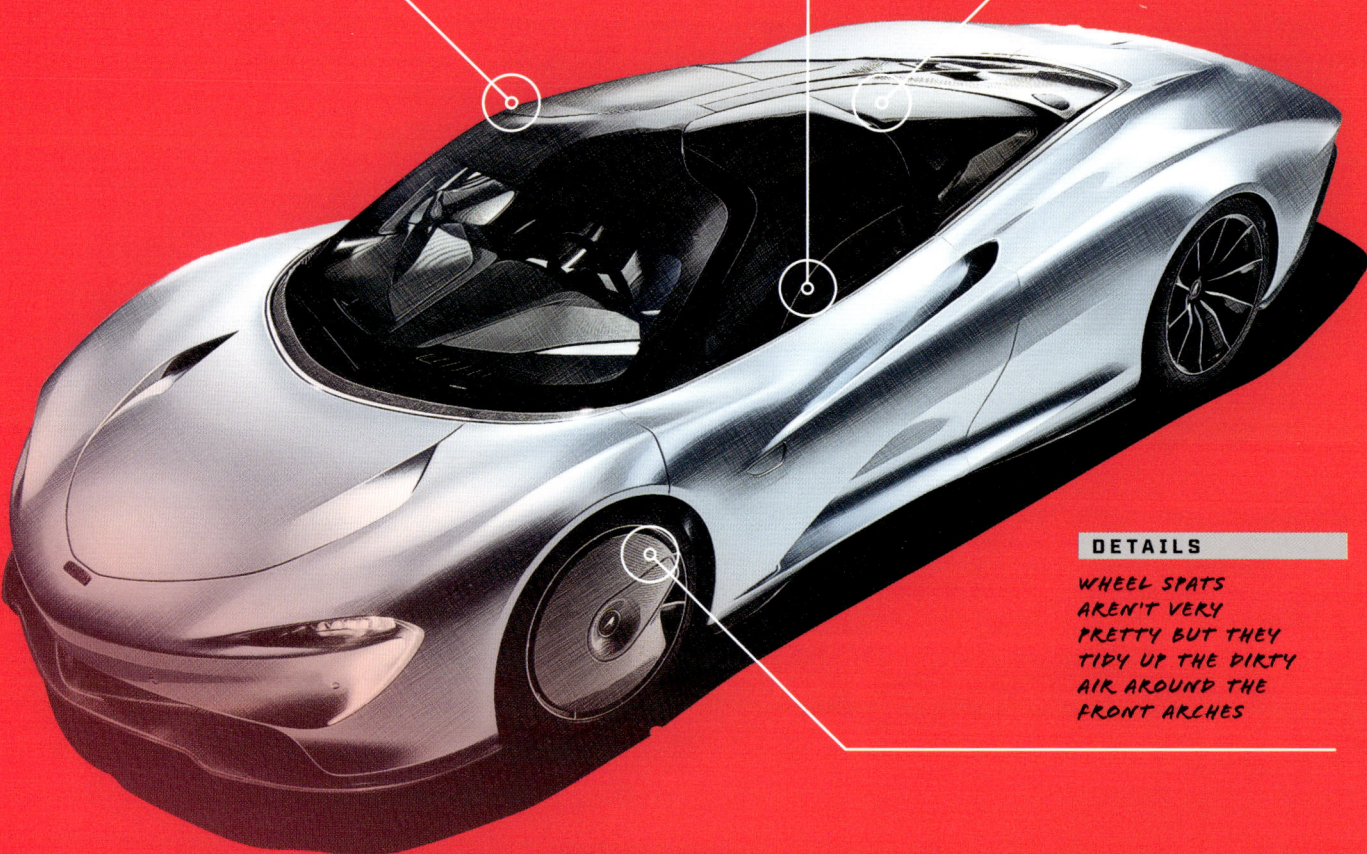

VEHICLE TYPE –
MID-ENGINED, REAR-WHEEL DRIVE COUPE

POWERTRAIN –
TWIN TURBOCHARGED, 4.0-LITRE V8, 731BHP WITH E-MOTOR (308BHP), TOTAL POWER OUTPUT 1,036BHP, 848LB FT @5,500–6,500RPM, 1.64 KWH LITHIUM ION BATTERY

WEIGHT: 1,430KG (DRY)

DIMENSIONS –
LENGTH: 5,130MM
WIDTH: 1,999MM
HEIGHT: 1,117MM

TRANSMISSION –
SEVEN-SPEED DUAL CLUTCH

PERFORMANCE –
TOP SPEED 250MPH (LIMITED)
0–62MPH 3.0 SECONDS
0–186MPH 13 SECONDS

BRAIN-FRAZZLING FACT:

AT THE VERY TIP OF THE SPEEDTAIL'S, ER, TAIL YOU'LL FIND FLEXIBLE CARBON FIBRE AILERONS. THEY'RE INTEGRATED INTO THE SINGLE-PIECE CARBON FIBRE CLAMSHELL THAT EXTENDS FROM THE REAR OF THE DOORS TO THE END OF THE CAR. THE AILERONS ARE PUSHED UP BY HYDRAULIC ACTUATORS TO A MAXIMUM OF 119MM, AND ARE PRIMARILY THERE TO BALANCE OUT THE AERODYNAMICS AT SPEED, BUT ALSO ACT AS AN AIR-BRAKE.

managing wheelspin in the first three gears. It smashes through 100mph in what must be around six seconds, but only when you're into fourth gear does the thing feel like it belongs to a speed category that makes the Ferrari 812 subjectively about as accelerative as a Fiat 500. It's absolutely savage – the temptation to stare at the rapid number changes on the speedometer is easily overcome by the need to look ahead, because it does wander a little bit as you approach 200mph. Nothing worrying, just a little looseness that would probably have Bugatti engineers yelling at each other and consulting laptops.

And it just keeps going. The combination of vast power pushing something so light and so slippery is utterly compelling. Perhaps the most intriguing and telling part of its behaviour is that when you do lift somewhere north of 220, the Speedtail doesn't slow down much at all. In a Chiron, the same driver input feels like you've smashed the brakes, such is the drag from its bodywork and wide tyres and the sheer friction and inertia of is vast all-wheel-drive chassis. The waif-like, rear-driven Speedtail glides with a serenity that makes you wonder if it might actually hit 200mph with just 300bhp.

We don't push beyond 225 because this car is one of those weathered and abused prototypes carmakers use to perfect the real thing. And also because we run out of runway. But the main question it leaves is why McLaren hasn't aimed for the higher top speed the Speedtail is so obviously capable of achieving. Then you remember some of the crazy engineering solutions Bugatti has developed to ensure its cars keep going beyond 260mph. On which basis, not only does McLaren's approach seem entirely wise, the subject doesn't seem to matter any more. Two-fifty is plenty for us and we suspect it's plenty for you, too.

If the styling is captivating, the message behind the Speedtail and how its maker imagines it being used is plain refreshing. This isn't a track car. There will be no talk of lap times and all that stuff – this is a road car, a grand touring super-machine in the mould of a Lamborghini Miura or Ferrari Daytona but extrapolated to a point where, if it were possible, it could travel as quickly as a light aircraft. This is the future we read about in Eighties car magazines, never mind the reality of a crumbling road network.

Does the three-seater arrangement actually work? Partially. Three six-footers will struggle to get comfortable – although we all know that large blokes shrink miraculously quickly when offered the chance to ride in something very special and very tiny. But those side berths are better suited to smaller humans. So we'd suggest that the ideal journey for the Speedtail is probably one piloted by a single, potentially raffish gentleman accompanied by two smaller female companions; dashing from, say, Gare du Nord to Antibes for something nice to eat and appropriate post-dinner entertainment.

Other orientations are equally well catered for, so long as the shotgunners are below 5ft 8in. So the schoolrun is an option too, although you probably don't need quite this level of performance for that task. Look, a conventionally configured GT is a more pragmatic solution, but who really cares? Anyone with the bunce to afford one in the first place will already have many toys capable of filling that role, and just a few minutes plonked bang in the middle of that cabin will be enough to dispel any concerns about passenger headroom. This car is graceful theatre on wheels.

We ought to talk about how it goes around corners, too. McLaren really only talks about the drag figure and the wheel spats that smooth airflow and the bendy rear wings that emerge at high speed, which is a bit worrying. The promotional discourse is all straight-line, so there was a worry that they'd forgotten about bends. We needn't have fretted. This is a slightly softened 720S underneath – a car so bloody talented it can easily spare 10 per cent of its agility and ultimate grip and still hand just about any other supercar its arse on a signed Jam album (obtuse Woking reference, that).

The horribly complicated hydraulic cross-linked suspension remains, as does the sense that sometimes it over-thinks road situations that don't require quite so much processor thought. But the ride is freakishly level, the grip is brilliant even in the wet and the steering offers weight and feel in quantities that modern Ferraris so sorely miss. It's a fun car to hustle and to slide – just be aware that at 5,137mm long, you need quite a lot of space when that tush arcs wide. Whack that and you'd get a massive bill.

Said tush actually contains a very generous boot, so the Speedtail is also practical. The ergonomics feel less so at first – the desire to keep the dash clean and symmetrical means that some buttons lurk underneath the dash itself, but also allows a bunch of switches to sit above the driver's head. And as we all know, fiddling about with a roof panel is only beaten in the cool stakes by, er, having a steering wheel in the middle. It underlines the Speedtail's position in the nonsense world of the hypercar, adds another element that marks this car out as something really very different indeed. It's also the most compelling car McLaren has made since the P1.

"IT'S A FUN CAR TO HUSTLE AND SLIDE. YOU NEED LOTS OF SPACE WHEN THE REAR ARCS WIDE"

12

WHY IT'S HERE
Because it takes an era-defining Mercedes F1 powertrain and installs it in a road legal car – with unexpected results

MERCEDES AMG ONE

Although its body design has stayed true to the original concept, every aspect of the One's exterior has been altered in order to meet Mercedes' stringent targets for the car

P romises and hindsight. Somewhere between them lies a truth that could surely help us all out. It might go something like this: don't overpromise, because if you fail to deliver you will be left with two potentially paralysing choices – hold your hands up and say you were too ambitious but that the potential glory was worth the risk of failure. Or just try to blag your way out of it. Most of us, of course, defer to the latter.

What does this have to do with a Mercedes sports car? The brand is still capable of brilliance, even if it has recently resorted to the kind of crowd-pleasing that undermines its amazing history. But the AMG One is something else again, no less than a genuine attempt to put a fiendishly complicated – and hugely successful – Mercedes Formula One powertrain into a road legal hypercar. There was a dash of JFK's famous, "We choose to … not because that will be easy, but because it will be hard" 1962 Apollo 11 speech about the Mercedes announcement back in 2017, a boldness that few of us could resist. But there is also the suspicion that the individual who made the decision to announce a road car with a Formula One engine hadn't asked the people who actually designed the F1 engine if such a project was even possible before going public with the plan. Given the use of a time machine, it's moot whether that individual would make the same decision again.

This is because the AMG One has become an industry case study in how painful car development can be. Stories of its troubled genesis have regularly filtered into conversations with engineers. And when we hear these stories as car obsessives, we

The One operates with three different aerodynamic modes: Highway, Race Max Downforce and Race DRS. The ducts and louvres on top of the front wheelarches adjust accordingly, and the rear wing is either open or retracted. The display, below, takes some figuring out

Left, the One is shod in bespoke Michelin Pilot Sport Cup 2R tyres. Do not drive over any potholes

have to decide whether to scoff at the apparent arrogance of promising something and failing to deliver it on time – remember the One is three years late – and then tweet about it not being fast enough. Or to double down on the belief that the boffins will be able to fix everything based on the general belief that the world is a better place with a Mercedes F1-engined hypercar in it. Who amongst us doesn't want the One to be great?

Off to the Nürburgring, then, to join a group of people lucky enough to sample a machine that has over 1,000bhp and active front wheelarch aerodynamics. We're given a brief overview of the car's controls by the project chief and then a crash course in the steering wheel and how you change the many chassis, powertrain and aero settings. All of which leaves us nodding confidently while inwardly thinking, "Didn't really get much of that."

The One is hugely complicated, perhaps the most complex car we've ever driven. It has so many different modes it's difficult to explain them all, but they are roughly split into road and track, whereupon the driver can then choose the level of performance versus battery depletion and ESP/traction intervention. There are nine settings of traction control alone and three modes of ESP. At least that's what we're told at the time, only to receive a message from someone a few hours after leaving the circuit telling us there's a *fourth* ESP setting called 'Pro'. Hmm. That might have been useful in what would turn out to be rather challenging circumstances.

A quick interlude now to explain just how complicated this car really is. At its heart sits a 1.6-litre single turbocharged V6. The turbo is effectively split between the intake and exhaust and this allows a 121bhp electric motor to sit between input and output. This is what F1 commentators call the MGU-H and it effectively reduces turbo lag. On the back of the internal combustion engine, which produces 566bhp, is a bigger 161bhp electric motor (MGU-K, to the aforementioned F1 commentators) and these both drive the rear axle. Each of the front wheels has a 161bhp electric motor, which F1 commentators don't have to worry about. Peak power is a claimed 1,049bhp and no torque figure has been published because it is too difficult to calculate. Given that half the work is undertaken by electrons, we can probably summarise it as "plenty".

The basic structure of the car is made from carbon fibre, as is the bodywork. The transmission is closely related to the F1 car's and it's built by Xtrac. The suspension is a complicated pushrod set-up and the car has substantial heaters to pre-warm the cats before start-up. Add to this a beautifully trimmed cabin, the usual suite of Mercedes luxuries and even an electric steering column, and you begin to understand how the One has bloated to a not inconsiderable 1,695kg.

That isn't enough to make its four-figure power output appear mean, but it does drag the car's power-to-weight ratio back into the clutches of less exotic machinery. Mercedes' claims of 0–62mph in 2.9secs, 0–124mph in 7.0secs and a 219mph maximum still seem pretty seismic, but they also make it no faster than a McLaren 765 LT. Having said that, the McLaren feels uncomfortably fast at times and it's reasonable to question how much faster a car needs to be, or indeed at which point we need to judge everything by how fast it is. After all, most £2m cars will get annihilated by a £35k motorcycle.

But back to the Nürburgring where the engineers and support crew for the One remain engaging but seem a little nervous. First up is a ducks and drakes learning session behind a GT Black Series driven by DTM motorsport legend and AMG ambassador Bernd Schneider. He explains that his tyres will take time to warm up then immediately sets off at a pace that would probably result in a decent qualifying position in a GT3 race.

There's a lot to take in here. We're in 'Race' mode, no aero deployed, but full power is available. The steering weight is delicious, the brake pedal feels weird, the noise is painful. That's right, the car everyone thought too quiet during its appearance at the Goodwood Festival of Speed is, from the inside, the loudest car we've ever driven – the V6 combining with all the other bits to produce something that burrows behind the eardrums into your skull. For the first half lap it's amusing, then it hurts. What else? The car understeers, but maybe that's just tyre temperature.

We pile down the main straight, the Black Series already holding up the hypercar, even with Bernd doing his usual mighty thing at the wheel. The One's transmission is in automatic mode and as it auto blips from third to second gear, the V6 suddenly cuts and a warning symbol flashes on the dash. Gliding to a stop, we radio Bernd and, as words are exchanged, the engine gargles back to life without the driver touching any button. Weird.

"THE ONE IS COMPLICATED, PERHAPS THE MOST COMPLEX CAR WE HAVE EVER DRIVEN"

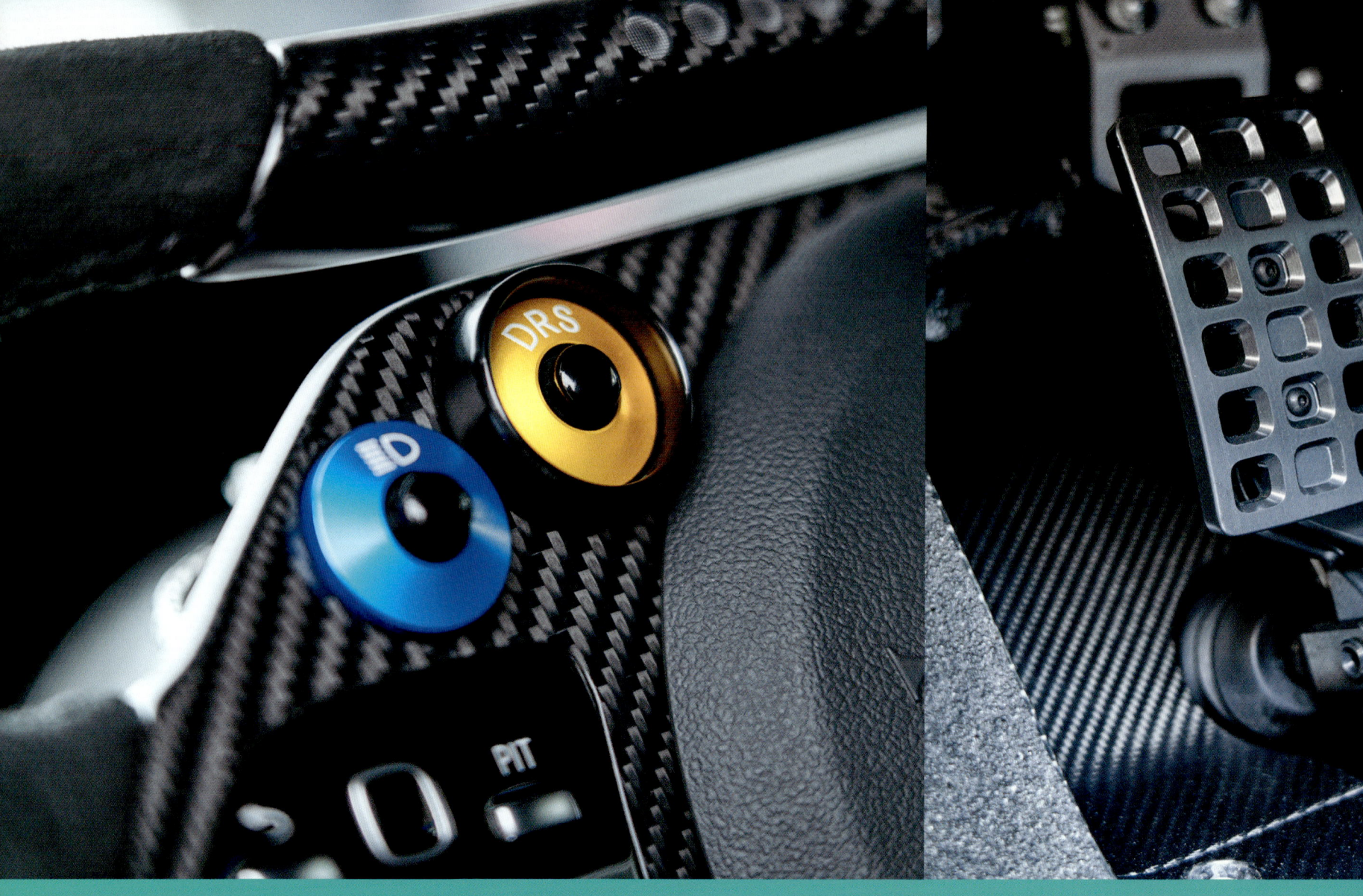

AMG One has six different driving modes: Race Safe, Race, EV, Individual, Race Plus and Strat 2, the last two of which are for track use only. Strat 2 adopts the most extreme aero and suspension settings, and summons all 1,049bhp…

Back in the pits, the laptops are out in force and the engaging AMG gentlemen are now grimacing a bit. We go back out again after 10 minutes, and the same thing happens halfway into the first lap when we really attack a braking zone and the engine uses all available revs for the downshift.

More laptops, a bit more head scratching, and then an engineer takes the car for a spin himself and rolls back into the pit lane with a forlorn look: "I have the same problem." The solution that is initially offered is to be more gentle on downshifts. But we'd been letting the car do those, so how could we be more gentle? "Maybe use gears one, two and three only?" Sorry, not really interested in doing that.

"He has been driving the car much harder than the others," says someone from Mercedes – it's no wonder yesterday's super influencer is so chummy with AMG. It would seem they just potter about in cars and watch as the "likes" come rolling in. A strange currency.

We have the beginnings of a stand-off. A Mercedes hypercar needs to be driven properly, as in flat-out. What's the point in driving it at 60 per cent? Are the 275 people paying £2.3 million for this thing going to be asked to do that? A second car that was to be used for some extra filming duties is nominated. Time ebbs away. So far we have completed one fast lap of the Nürburgring GP circuit.

This, er, One, is a little more "development" – a little rougher. Halfway around the first lap the car hits 90mph and a speed limiter cuts in, with a warning about aero parts coming up on the dash. Another laptop session and now some very furrowed German brows. The issue is a sensor on the rear spoiler that isn't communicating well with some control unit – a fix is made, tested and doesn't work. Then someone concludes that if the car runs in 'Race' mode with all the spoilers already deployed, the speed limiter won't need to get all shirty. And they're right, because the car zings around an entire lap with no further issues.

208
SPECIFICATION

POWERTRAIN
1.6-LITRE TURBO V6 PRODUCES 566BHP AT 9,000RPM, BOOSTED BY FOUR ELECTRIC MOTORS; ONE IS ON THE ENGINE, ANOTHER SITS BETWEEN THE TURBO AND COMPRESSOR, THE FINAL TWO ARE ON THE FRONT AXLE

SUSPENSION
PUSHROD SET-UP USES FIVE-LINK DESIGN FRONT AND REAR. CERAMIC BALL BEARINGS IN WHEELS REDUCE FRICTION

TRANSMISSION
DRIVE IS VIA A HYDRAULICALLY OPERATED SEVEN-SPEED AUTOMATED MANUAL WITH A FOUR-DISC CLUTCH

CHASSIS
AMG ONE HAS CARBON MONOCOQUE WITH A LARGE REAR SUBFRAME TO SUPPORT THE POWERTRAIN

VEHICLE TYPE –
MID-ENGINED, ALL-WHEEL DRIVE COUPE

POWERTRAIN –
1.6-LITRE V6, TURBOCHARGED WITH FOUR ELECTRIC MOTORS. COMBUSTION ENGINE POWER OUTPUT 566BHP, ELECTRIC MOTOR OUTPUT 603BHP. OVERALL COMBINED POWER OUTPUT 1,049BHP @ 9,000RPM, TORQUE FIGURE NOT POSSIBLE DUE TO COMPLEXITY OF DRIVETRAIN

WEIGHT: 1,695KG (DRY)

DIMENSIONS –
LENGTH: 4,750MM
WIDTH: 2,006MM
HEIGHT: 1,270MM

TRANSMISSION –
SEVEN-SPEED AUTOMATED MANUAL GEARBOX

PERFORMANCE –
TOP SPEED 219 MPH 0-62MPH 2.9 SECONDS
0-186MPH 15.6 SECONDS

BRAIN-FRAZZLING FACT:

ALTHOUGH ITS POWERTRAIN IS DERIVED FROM F1, THE AMG ONE'S AERODYNAMIC PACKAGE IS CLOSER IN CONFIGURATION TO THE COMPANY'S GT3 RACE CARS. EVERY HOT SPOT, THE BATTERY, PUMPS AND COMBUSTION SYSTEM ARE PROVIDED WITH FRESH AIR, A REQUIREMENT THAT GOES BEYOND THE BODY OF THE CAR. DETAIL IS EVERYTHING: EVEN THE CONNECTING PILLAR FOR THE DOOR MIRROR IS SPECIFICALLY CURVED TO REDUCE DRAG, TO OPTIMISE AERO ACOUSTICS AND TO ENHANCE REAR DOWNFORCE.

Forget everything you've experienced from a normal super/hypercar powertrain. This may not be the fastest thing out there, but it's intense and plain wonderful and, crucially, unique. The engine is frantic above 9,000rpm, but upchanges sound slovenly, albeit without any sense of acceleration being clipped. Turns out some KERS is deployed between changes to sustain momentum. The chassis is supple in 'Race' mode, but firm as hell in 'Race Plus'. All we can prise from the car is understeer – whatever we try to do, the front pushes and the rear axle seems to have crazy traction. The noise is now too invasive, so earplugs are definitely required. Time to concentrate on the brakes, which have a full suite of regenerative technology in them. They really aren't easy – the initial thump of deceleration is logical, but keeping them on the edge of the ABS from 100mph to hairpin speed is tricky.

And that must have something to do with the driving position, which is just plain odd. How a ground-up design ends up with barely enough legroom for someone 5ft 7in tall is a mystery, one that taller AMG One owners may soon be irritated to ponder. Added to which is the fact that the bucket seat hewn from the chassis has very little lateral support. It's bizarre – nearly as bizarre as fitting a weedy audio system to the world's loudest car. And a Bluetooth phone. Honestly, don't even bother.

And yet the AMG One is utterly intriguing. We strongly suspect one of the most interesting and rewarding cars ever made might lurk under all that, dare we say it, not quite finished technology. ESP Pro? It's fair to say that our first drive did not go smoothly. Not only were additional drive modes revealed after the event, but we were later told about a chassis calibration that eradicates all that understeer we experienced. So what *can* we conclude? Well, the F1 motor is beguiling, the car itself looks amazing in the flesh, and we adore what it represents. But it's also easy to think that the whole five-year struggle to get the thing to this point has been so traumatic that the company just wants to deliver the cars and move on to simpler tasks. Nuclear fission, perhaps.

This, then, will be remembered as one of the great automotive follies, but also one of the most fascinating machines ever made. Back to the question we posed at the beginning of this story. Did Mercedes hold up its hands, or try to blag it? Probably a bit of both, in truth.

But for the most part, the AMG One confirms what we've always suspected – that the greatest cars aren't always objectively very good.

"THE NOISE IS SO INVASIVE THAT EAR PLUGS ARE DEFINITELY REQUIRED"

Below, an F1-style rectangular steering wheel has rotary controls for the drive modes and gearchange shift lights (and an airbag). Pedal box is adjustable, rear view is handled by a camera. Right, cooling on this car is a major consideration

13

WHY IT'S HERE
Like a steampunk emissary from an imagined future-past, Pagani mixes all sorts of elements to create a glorious new whole

PAGANI UTOPIA

Above, the adaptive suspension is by British specialist Tractive and is fantastically compliant. The engine is based on a 6.0-litre Mercedes-AMG V12. Gearbox, right, is a seven speed manual from Xtrac. Tyres, below left, are from Pirelli

Right, the Utopia's interior is utterly unlike anything else out there. It's cluttered and busy, but in a deeply satisfying way. Metal, leather, levers, dials, switches... it's a hypercar fever dream. And when you turn the engine off, a violin exit tune – written by Horacio Pagani – is played

Where to start? It's a toss up between wing mirror and gearbox. And the weather. But let's go with the initial plan and tell you about the side mirror. Because look at it. It's more steampunk street lamp than functional item. Wonderful, but needlessly elaborate.

Welcome to the world of the Pagani Utopia – a Jules Verne fever dream for the 23rd century. Done with the mirror? Then have a look at those bonkers carbon wheel spats, the brake calipers like bronze knuckle dusters, the elegant slivers of aluminium, the leather buckles, the roof portholes. It's a 1930s vision of the far future, Flash Gordon's motor conveyance. Pagani likes to claim its cars perfectly balance art and science, but walk around it and the more you will be convinced it's all about the art, the sculpture, the effortless luxury, certain that functionality has been willingly overlooked, that Pagani has let the weight swell unacceptably.

And then you drive it.

The ride is supple and composed, the Utopia calm in the driver's hands, the clutch easy, the motor tractable, the manners polished. Later, we'll discover how sharp and fizzy the twin turbo V12 is, that there's an animal contained within. Later still, the roads will finally dry out, giving the Utopia a chance to demonstrate its eager, tenacious front end, suspension finesse

Left, yes there are three pedals in the Utopia, and they're as beautifully produced as every other component in this amazing machine. Below, bespoke luggage too

Left, sitting inside the Utopia is like being positioned inside a giant watch mechanism

and rampant, explosive, exponential acceleration.

Those mirrors. There's no wind noise. No flex at speed. They're well positioned for visibility, the reflective area is big and, when you park, they pivot on gorgeous aluminium base plates, twisting in to make themselves slightly less vulnerable. They work flawlessly. They're still perfectly useful in the thumping rain and thick spray we're currently enduring. But we've got it easy. Cars coming the other way are shedding snow from their roofs. We call a halt to our plan to head further and higher; £2.22 million cars whose only contact patches with the already treacherous surface are track-focused, ready-chilled Pirelli Corsa tyres, clearly need to be afforded plenty of respect. Already there have been spits of wheelspin as 811lb ft of torque bombardment is hurled at the traction control's defences.

But they're robust, and the Utopia is fluent. The accelerator's responses are perfectly calibrated. There is also a manual gearbox. That's right. No tricks or special technology here, this is a three-pedal Pagani. With a seven speed gearbox that starts with a dog leg and is four planes wide. We've driven Astons with this gear layout and wished for an auto (you can have this as an auto if you want, but only 25 per cent of owners are). We're not saying this has been developed by choirs of angels and divine intervention, but the shift is far sweeter and lighter than it has any right to be. Horacio and his merry band of artisans have surely done something very clever with the self-centring – it seems to intuitively pause momentarily on the second/third plane when you're in low gears.

"INFLUENCE HAS COME FROM ALL OVER: ART DECO, SCIENCE FICTION, VICTORIANA. IT'S A GENIUS FUSION"

We can't help glancing down at the gearlever as we've headed for the hills. Not because we're struggling to negotiate its maze, but to watch the lever row back and forth, view the linkages, see it slide and glide through the open gate. It's a work of – yes – art. And engineering. And science. And also collaboration. Because the gearbox itself comes from British company Xtrac, which counts GMA and Red Bull amongst its clients.

The GMA T.50 is a very different car. That's taut, direct and snarling. This is more relaxed and flamboyant. Both are hugely occupying cars to drive, the T.50 for the tactility of its controls, the Utopia for the tactility of your surroundings. It's like driving a Baroque theatre. No matter what's happening outside, where you're driving or what the weather's like, your peripheral vision flutters and dances with whirring dials, preposterous airvents, ornate metalwork, levers and leather, carbon and toggles.

Horacio Pagani is not a follower of professional tidy-upper Marie Kondo. Every inch of the cockpit has something to draw your eye, tease your senses, distract and compel. It is cluttered with luxury and drips with decadence. Is it all a bit much? Occasionally, yes, but it's never frustrating, it's not like having to battle with a touchscreen. There is a single screen, elbowing its way to prominence between the two glorious main dials. Operated by clickwheel, it does pack masses of functionality (including Carplay) into not much real estate. Ergonomically it's wonderful. The seat cossets, the driving position is just so, there's masses of steering adjustment and it's easy to position the car on the road despite the heavily curved windscreen. You can even see a little bit out the back through the craftily positioned mirror and window.

Mostly though, the Utopia's cabin is like being inside a watch mechanism, seeing needles and dials and levers flick about. It's a more mechanical, connected experience than expected because so much is on display and usually mounted on a metal plinth. Pretty much every bit of metal you can see was machined from aluminium billet by Pagani themselves. That runs to some 777 components across the whole car. The steering wheel started life as a Cheddar cheese-sized 47kg lump, machined over 30 hours down to 1.7kg. As ever, these back stories only enrich the experience.

It's the same outside. You want to get up close and pore over it, learn what's been done and why. But when you step back, the news is more challenging. The Utopia isn't a pretty car; the front end is too busy, the glass area looks a bit sunken and hooded. But the rear is fabulous, with that low centre deck, the rear wing elements forming the oval shape of the Pagani logo, the lights that hover in the Zonda-esque heat extractor housings.

Besides, Paganis have always been a little overwrought, bordering on fussy. It's what helps make them so charismatic and distinctive to look at.

Above, note the snow in the picture. The Pagani Utopia demands respect, but never more so than in sub-optimal weather conditions

And remember, they're built in such low volumes, and are in such demand (all 99 initial Utopias were spoken for a year before anyone knew what it looked like), that Horacio is free to cut loose, do what he likes. No need to follow fashion or current trends when your clients trust you to this degree.

Rain puddles either side of the centre exhaust tremble to the V12's bass beat. The basic AMG-sourced 6.0-litre engine is carried over, but it's changed a lot since the early days of the Huayra, where the turbos made it breathy and robbed it of music and character. Don't worry that it only revs to 6,700rpm. This is an object lesson in how to create drama and excitement without revs. Up these hillside roads we climb, and the engine is sharp, reactive. You can sense how light the pistons and crankshaft must be from how eagerly it responds before the turbos get going. They introduce themselves quietly, predictably, but when they start whistling, brace yourself because that's when the runaway reaction starts, this whumping impact of bottomless torque forcing itself on only 1,340kg of body mass (including fluids). The first few times it happens, your brain struggles to keep up, to the extent that you find yourself lifting off, giggling, relieved that it's over.

Deep bass thrum, fizzing turbos and an insistent howl give the Utopia a brutal background theme, overlaid by the V12's smooth howl. The effect is at once soothing and alarming. It's much the same to drive, although that's principally due to the anti-hypercar conditions. To be honest it's a miracle Pagani even let us out of the factory gates this morning. There are pools of water around that could see the Utopia doing a very passable impression of Captain Nemo's famous submarine.

We get away from the valley by heading up the tight, pitted SP26. In places the whole road is collapsed and slumping off the hillsides and it's the nearest we get to removing the Utopia from its otherwise broad comfort zone. The diff is tight around hairpins, traction is easily overcome, the nose is occasionally sniffy for cambers. But the sense of driving something richly rewarding and fabulously tactile is overwhelming. Even if you can pick "faults". The inverted commas are deliberate because we're sure this is exactly the car as Pagani intends. The steering has a fast rack, turns quickly and precisely into corners, but it isn't the last word in writhing

224
SPECIFICATION

DESIGN
Although Pagani is a materials genius, the main man is also a true artist when it comes to body design

CHASSIS
Pagani is the king of exotic composites. Carbo-Titanium and Carbo-Triax are used on the Utopia, with Cr-Mo alloy in the subframes

ENGINE
Engine is a 6.0-litre twin turbo V12 sourced from Mercedes-AMG. Good for 852bhp and 811lb ft of torque

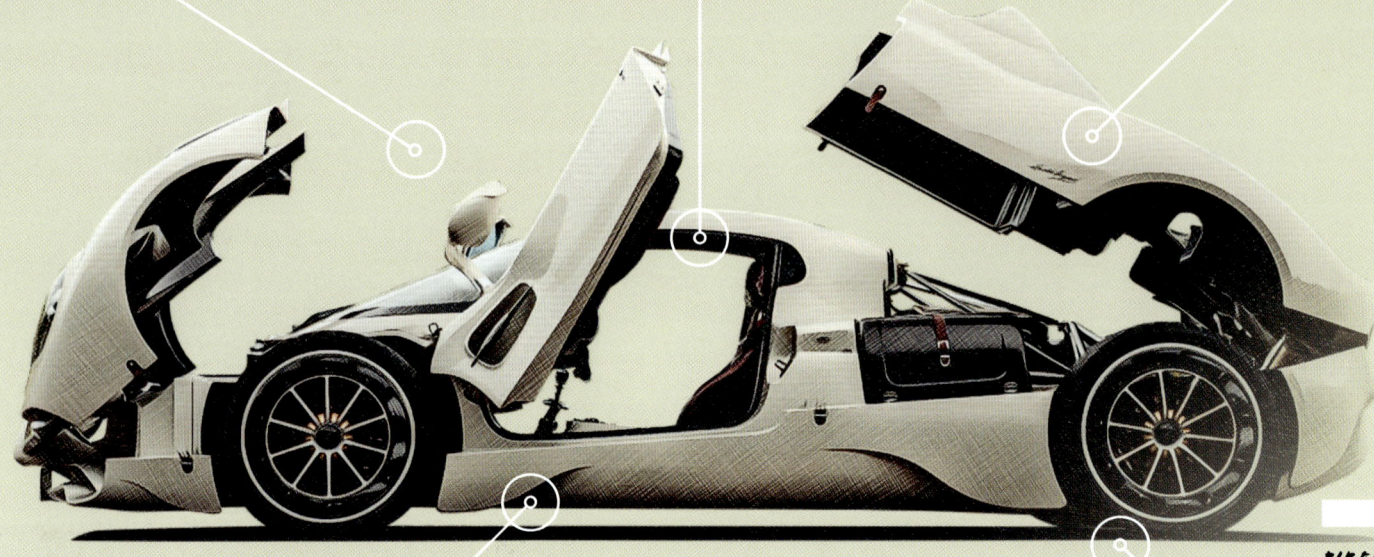

STRUCTURE
Utopia is globally homologated, passes California's ultra strict crash test regulations

TYRES
Pirelli P Zero Corsas, 325/30 R22s at the rear. But you can have Sottozeros for low temperature conditions

VEHICLE TYPE –
Mid-engined, rear-wheel drive coupe

POWERTRAIN –
Pagani developed 6.0-litre twin turbo (based on Mercedes-AMG unit)
852bhp V12, 811lb ft @ 2,800–5,900rpm

WEIGHT: 1,280kg (dry)

DIMENSIONS –
LENGTH: 4,957mm
WIDTH: 2,037mm
HEIGHT: 1,169mm

TRANSMISSION –
Seven-speed manual by Xtrac

PERFORMANCE –
Top speed 218mph
0–62mph 3.1 seconds (estimated)

225 BRAIN-FRAZZLING FACT(S):

PAGANI HAS DEVELOPED ITS OWN COMPOSITES FOR THE UTOPIA. THEY'RE CALLED CARBO-TITANIUM AND CARBO-TRIAX, AND ARE USED IN THE CAR'S MAIN TUB, ROOF AND INTERIOR. ALL THE WORK IS DONE IN-HOUSE BY THE COMPANY'S ARTISAN ENGINEERS. THEN THERE'S ITS USE OF ALUMINIUM. FOR EXAMPLE, THE STEERING WHEEL BEGINS LIFE AS 43KG OF SOLID ALUMINIUM BILLET, WHICH IS MILLED DOWN TO JUST 1.7KG.

"SITTING INSIDE THE UTOPIA IS LIKE BEING IN A MINIATURISED BAROQUE THEATRE. THERE IS NO CENTRAL SCREEN IN HERE"

Right, note the gearshift's exposed mechanism and the flamboyant interior

feedback. Similarly, the gearshift is ever so slightly rubbery and the Brembo brakes only show their teeth once you're properly into their travel. This, we suspect, is because Pagani wants the Utopia to relax its driver, to make them feel in control, not have them all tense and edgy because they're bombarded by signals. So it filters those signals. Not too much, just enough to remove intimidation and fidget from the equation.

When the roads do finally start to dry, it's like opening the door to a new world. The detectable rigidity of the Carbo-Titanium and Carbo-Triax (we are not making these words up) tub contrasts with the sure control and compliance of the adaptive Tractive suspension. It never loses its sense of calm, even when being hurled forward with outright violence. As a result, the Utopia doesn't feel nervy or highly strung – not what you'd have thought by looking at it. Very rarely do we feel the need to press the Super Soft button on the dash, where in most Ferraris it's the first thing you would look for. As with everything else the Utopia does, it rides expensively, luxuriously.

It's easy to think of the Utopia as a trinket, a play thing. But this is a fully globally homologated hypercar. It's been endlessly crash tested, through WLTP emissions (18.7mpg and 342g/km in case you're wondering), passes California's stringent regs. Pagani is rightfully proud of that, because it's a reminder that the engineering has been as lovingly crafted as the design. That's what we see – and all most of us will ever get to experience. But what's been true of Pagani since the Zonda arrived 25 years ago is that they know exactly how to create soulful, magical, impossibly special cars.

This, putting all else aside, is a driver's hypercar. It just delivers its thrills across a wider band than most. A Bugatti Chiron is as beautifully assembled as this, but way heavier, less thrilling and alert. The GMA T.50 takes that side much further but lacks the Utopia's dramatic sense of theatre. Ultimately, each is a distillation of the people that created it, and you could argue that where supercars are about driving, hypercars are about offering additional levels to their "performance". This is not so easy to quantify, because it isn't just about speed and numbers. Here you need to think about performance as artistic expression: the Utopia isn't about driving performance, it's about the performance of driving. It's something we believe it does above and beyond any rival. Viewed that way, this new Utopia is the hypercar's hypercar. A utopia indeed. With steampunk wing mirrors.

Right, the Utopia looks somehow even more artful with water sluicing off its body

 #14

WHY IT'S HERE
Because it's a Red Bull creation designed by Adrian Newey, an F1-infused hypercar for people who aren't Max Verstappen...

RED BULL RB17

On the day we meet Adrian Newey for an exclusive preview of the £5.75m RB17, he's just back from the Miami Grand Prix, a race weekend that convulsed with the confirmation that he was departing Red Bull. Formula One's technical figures tend to be shadowy boffins, rarely discussed outside the nerdier motorsport websites or publications. Yet Newey is a household name, mostly because the cars he designs are incredibly effective when it comes to winning races. In F1, his cars have chalked up 12 constructors' and 13 drivers' titles, designs for Williams, McLaren and Red Bull that have been elegantly ingenious interpretations of whatever regulations were extant. He can visualise air flow, it's said, has complex equations floating before his eyes like the physicists in the brainy Netflix hit *3 Body Problem*.

And now we have the RB17. This is the fabled creature that has occupied his thoughts since 2020, but whose origins lie much further back. Neither a road car nor a competition machine, it's a track-only hypercar that marshals almost everything Newey has learned in his 40-plus years career, a maximal motor car conceived without constraint, other than the ones he and the development team have imposed on themselves. It's Newey unplugged or turned up to 11, depending on your preferred musical analogy. For that alone it has every granule of our attention. That and the presence of a Red Bull-spec, Cosworth-made 1,000bhp 4.5-litre V10 that can rev to 15,000rpm, in a car with an overall target weight of 875kg. And it has an e-motor.

We see it before the man himself arrives to guide us around it. First impressions? It looks big and surprisingly long, a space-age spaceship of a thing. It's mesmerising in detail and execution, and there's a clear visual through-line to a contemporary F1 car. Imagine a cockpit on a recent Red Bull and you're halfway there. Its side pods are sensational; hell, it's a non-

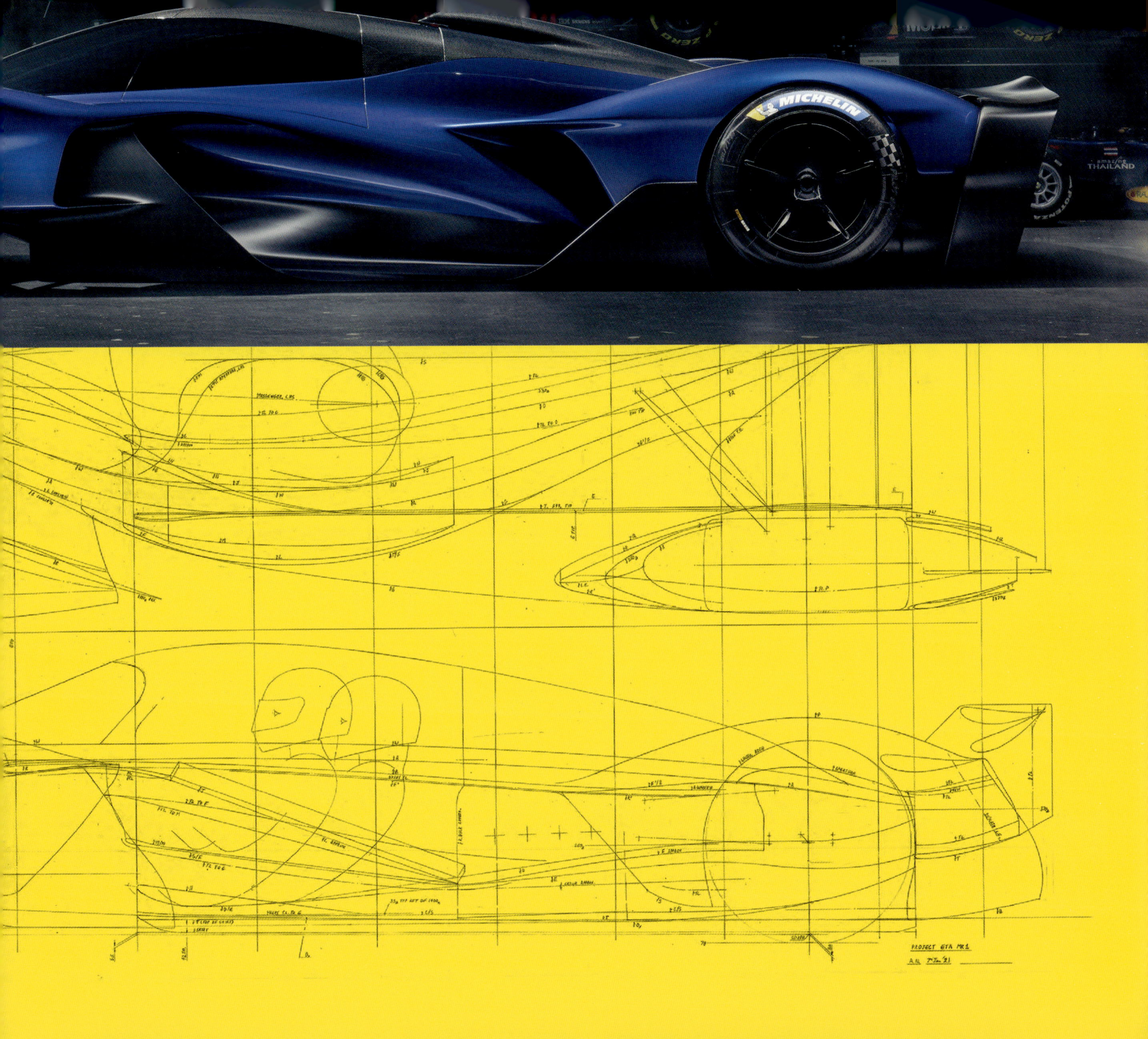

Left, RB17 pulses with Formula One technology. Hardly a surprise given who has presided over its creation. Opposite, Adrian Newey with some of his greatest hits

competition car that actually *has* side pods. It's also a shape that's defined more by what's missing than what's actually there. Porosity, they call it in the trade, and there are whole sections of the RB17 that invite you to go for a digital (as in hands and fingers) exploration of its open spaces.

In the old days, you might caress a car's surfaces, but you can't caress something that's not actually there. You can only imagine turbulent air around the front wheel arches being tidied up, before being redirected under the car and into a tunnel of stunning complexity. There are two fans in there somewhere, too, transforming all this energised air into aero magic. There's also a full-width rear wing that's there primarily to extract the air from the diffuser. The name? When Covid interrupted everything, Red Bull never ran an F1 car called RB17. Now the lost badge has a home.

Newey's, erm, news isn't the only elephant in the room (a room full of old Red Bull F1 cars). Form invariably follows function on a car like this, and the similarity to the Aston Martin Valkyrie is undeniable. That, of course, was another Newey project, a Red Bull-led collaboration that ran adrift when Aston went its own way in F1 under new owner, Lawrence Stroll. Estranged from one of its parents, the Valkyrie impressed mightily but felt under-developed and unfinished in some areas. It was also compromised because it was chasing downforce and mega lap times while also having to be road legal. An angel dancing on the head of a pin, some thought, even if the sight of one

"THE RB17 IS THE FABLED MACHINE THAT HAS OCCUPIED ADRIAN NEWEY'S THOUGHTS ON AND OFF SINCE 2010"

mixing in with ordinary traffic is more than enough to make your week.

The RB17's laser-precise track focus circumvents most philosophical queries. This is an Adrian Newey-designed car that will deliver F1 lap times and outrageous levels of driver engagement around the world's great crucibles of speed, places like Silverstone, Spa and Suzuka. That ought to be enough, right? As we're poring over some design sketches in an ante-room, the man himself arrives. His primary focus between now and his early 2025 departure from this hugely successful racing operation will be the RB17. Red Bull's Advanced Technologies division is fast-growing, but it's not a car manufacturer in any traditional sense of the term. This points to a steep learning curve, even for these guys. F1 teams don't exactly churn out cars, and consider that Red Bull Racing has made fewer than 100 chassis in its 20-year history. In other words, there is much work to be done.

"Good to see you again," Adrian says, to which I reply, "How was your weekend?" before immediately regretting it and mumbling incoherently. The man had media trailing after him the entire time, his departure another twist in a saga that has engulfed the world champions this season. "Oh, you know," he says with a weary smile. "Busy…"

On to the RB17. Remember the Red Bull X1, the wild-looking car that Newey designed for *GranTurismo 5* and *GT6*, back in 2010? Well, there was more to it than perhaps we thought at the time. "It was a fantasy car," Newey concedes. "It didn't have any CFD (computational fluid dynamics) or internal work. It was a first sketch that got turned into a styling model for a computer game. But it had the basic thought behind it, and it's been gently ticking away in the back of my mind since then."

The real thing reappeared on his radar in Christmas 2019. During a ski break, and frustrated by the lack of decent snow, Newey began drawing a

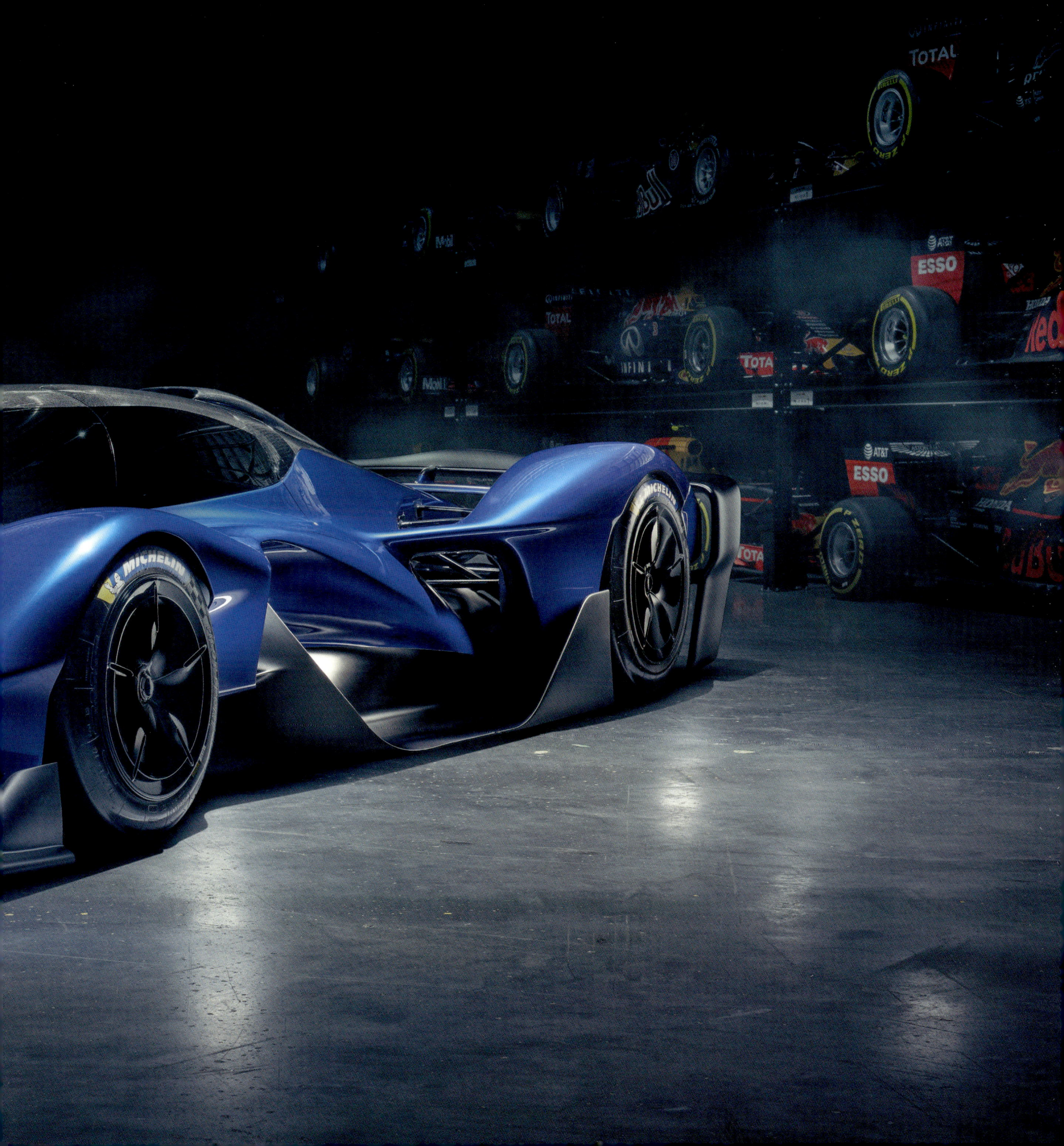

hypercar. For a man whose successes have been measured by one primary criteria – the stopwatch – you might be surprised by the principles he laid down for what would become the RB17.

"It's my belief that cars at this level should be something you can treat as a piece of art or sculpture," he explains. "My career has always been performance oriented, so when it comes to aerodynamics you always go with what makes the car faster. With this we wanted it to be a more rounded product in terms of the look, sound and the driving experience. The intent is the most important thing to start with. And that was to create a car that was capable of F1 lap times but at the same time be accessible to people – two people at that."

Turns out that Newey the technocrat is also democratic, and he insisted on broadening the RB17's remit. "I do track days from time to time and it's nice to be able to give passenger rides," he says evenly. "Take away the art side and this has to be about the enjoyment of the owner. It would be an even faster – and easier – project if it was a single-seater but I wanted it to be a two seater."

He continues: "There have been two seater F1 cars but they're not a very pleasant experience. With this car you've got proper visibility, and the passenger seat is slightly staggered. It makes sense to do it that way and it's an elegant solution. The wider cabin has weight and aerodynamic implications, but it was a penalty I felt we should take. There's luggage space at the front, space for two sets of overalls, and room for a pair of helmets behind you."

Whoever gets to experience it will have much to enjoy, though they might need to work on their neck muscles and resting heart rate. The RB17 really is a mildly civilised F1 car, better in some key respects, in fact. The chassis is made of carbon composite, as you'd expect. To be more technical about it, it's made from plies of woven cloth reinforced with uni-directional fibres to tailor the structural properties and give phenomenal structural integrity. The car also uses active suspension, banned in F1 since 1994, but core to the RB17's amazing bandwidth because it offers such precise control over the vehicle dynamics.

"You need a platform the active systems can work against," Rob Gray, RBAT's boss, explains. "We ran a lot of simulations to determine the minimal stiffness that still gave a good response on the active suspension system. We did find there's a point where it falls off a cliff. We're definitely ahead of that point. We could have made the car stiffer but it wouldn't have gone any faster. We got to a level that gave us the handling characteristics we wanted, beyond which extra stiffness just meant excess weight."

Safety is also a vital component. The RB17 takes its cues here from LMPH regulations, in terms of structural integrity but also significantly in what's called the "overturning moment". In essence, it shouldn't suffer from such an acute degree of lift in the event of an accident or impact that it becomes fully airborne (YouTube is full of examples of endurance racing cars doing this, before the new regs kicked in). The team has managed to comply with these restrictions without destroying the styling. Newey is passionate that the RB17 looks as good as possible, rather than turning into a misbegotten science experiment.

"On the parts of the F1 car I've drawn, and that's by no means all of it these days, the aesthetic part of the brain does kick in, maybe even subconciously," he says. "Very often the aerodynamically efficient form is also aesthetically pleasing. The Spitfire wasn't drawn for styling, or Concorde, but they were two of the prettiest aircraft that have ever been built." The process here is fascinating. Newey drew the aerodynamic surfaces, as ever by hand, which were transferred into CFD in order to visualise the air flow and understand the loads that were being generated. At that point, Red Bull hired a couple of RCA automotive design graduates to flesh out the surfaces, before submitting their proposals for more CFD analysis. If downforce points were lost during the styling process, the aero

"IT'S MY BELIEF THAT CARS AT THIS LEVEL SHOULD BE SOMETHING AKIN TO A PIECE OF ART OR SCULPTURE"

guys could suggest ways of recovering them. These loops would continue until everyone was happy, an iterative process that would obviously never happen in F1 because beauty is a by-product rather than a target requirement.

So the RB17 is a sculpture. No doubt there are wealthy people out there who would buy one purely for static display, but really that would be a monumental waste of Red Bull's first-class mental firepower. Nevertheless, how do you make something capable of delivering contemporary F1 lap times accessible to mere mortals? The active suspension is key here, as is a graduated traction control system and a range of chassis modes. Their parameters are still being configured, but Newey is clearly chuffed that active suspension is back in play.

"It allows you to change the mechanical balance and your stability margin," he explains with a flourish. "Combined with the car's active aero surfaces it allows you to change the centre of pressure [the ratio of front downforce versus rear downforce], which is quite far forwards in any case. And we will have knobs in the cockpit that allow you to do that on the fly, so you can have more stability on the entry to a low speed corner or more stability at the apex of a high speed one… it gives us tremendous flexibility."

The RB17 is targeting 1,700kg of downforce at 150mph. And what of the tyres, perhaps *the* limiting factor when it comes to such vast aero forces? Red Bull is working with Michelin on three different compounds. The most extreme tyre is the "confidential", which Newey says is a bit peaky but offers huge grip. The standard slick serves up more slip angle and is less temperature sensitive, and there will also be a treaded option. On the subject of slip angles, note that you're

looking in the wrong place if it's flamboyant power-sliding you're after. "Absolutely not," Newey says with a headmasterly tone. "I do not want to see any photos with all that going on. I know that's what you love but it leaves me cold, I must admit. It's just showboating, isn't it?"

Not that the man who races a Ford GT40 and Lotus 49B in historic events is averse to a car moving around beneath the driver. He understands interaction. "That's why we're offering all these different modes and tyre solutions. I wouldn't suggest [the RB17] is the first car you ever take on a race track, but if you turn out to have a lot of drive and determination, then you can get to extreme levels of performance. It has that adaptability."

The gearbox is a single barrel sequential designed and assembled in-house, although the gears themselves are made by a partner. Shift times will be fast, though not as fast as the instant-shift set up in an F1 car, to avoid excessive harshness. The e-motor takes care of first and reverse, and helps low speed manoeuvring, as well as adding 200bhp and torque-filling when

The RB17's rear view is dominated by the diffuser, and its aero requirements largely dictate its form. But Adrian Newey was adamant that the car also worked as a piece of pure design

242

SPECIFICATION

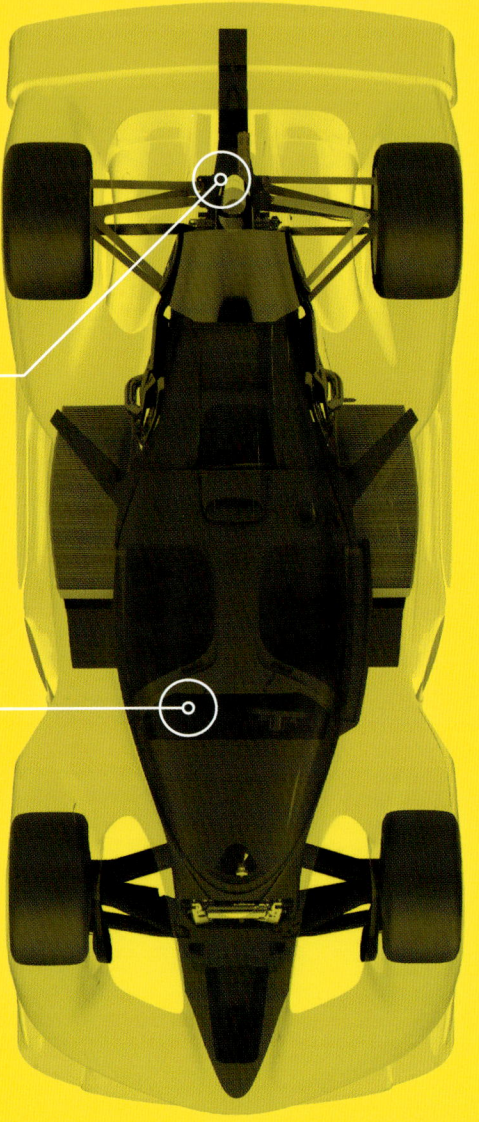

ENGINE
COSWORTH SUPPLIED V10 PRODUCES 1,000BHP BUT IS AIDED HERE BY A 200BHP E-MOTOR

BODY
RB17 IS CLOSER TO A CLOSED COCKPIT F1 CAR THAN LMPH, USES THE LATEST UNI-DIRECTIONAL CARBON FIBRE

DESIGN
TWO SEAT CONFIGURATION AND SAFETY WERE THE TWO BIGGEST CONSTRAINTS RB17 FACED IN DESIGN

AERO
RB17 HAS THE FULL PANOPLY OF AERO DEVICES, INCLUDING PHENOMENAL TUNNEL AND DIFFUSER, TWO FANS, CLEVER SIDE PODS AND FULL WIDTH REAR WING TO EXTRACT AIR

VEHICLE TYPE –
MID-ENGINED COUPE, REAR-WHEEL DRIVE

POWERTRAIN –
4.5-LITRE COSWORTH V10, 1000BHP, CAN REV TO 15,000RPM, PLUS 200BHP E-MOTOR

WEIGHT: SUB-900KG

DIMENSIONS –
LENGTH: 5,092MM
WIDTH: 2,060MM
HEIGHT: 1,055MM

TRANSMISSION –
SIX-SPEED SINGLE CLUTCH SEQUENTIAL

PERFORMANCE –
TOP SPEED 217MPH (LIMITED)
0-62MPH 2.4 SECS

243

BRAIN-FRAZZLING FACT:

THE RB17 USES ACTIVE SUSPENSION, WHICH WORKS IN TANDEM WITH THE CAR'S AERODYNAMIC SURFACES TO ALTER THE CENTRE OF PRESSURE. THIS IS THE RATIO OF DOWNFORCE, FRONT TO REAR, THAT AFFECTS THE STABILITY MARGIN AND THE OVERALL MECHANICAL BALANCE. THE DRIVER WILL BE ABLE TO ADJUST THE AERO SET-UP ON THE MOVE USING CONTROLS IN THE COCKPIT, DEPENDING ON THE CORNER AND REQUIREMENT.

required. In a similar vein, lessons have been learned from the painfully loud Valkyrie, so the V10 is a semi-stressed member rather than being bolted directly to the chassis. Compliantly mounting the engine added several kg but it was a price worth paying. The RB17 also has to meet the noise regulations of as many circuits as possible, and should be hitting no more than 105db. The exhaust is a 10-into-one set-up, inspired by 2000's Newey-designed McLaren MP4/15, a car he cites as the best-sounding F1 car of all. Its steering is fully hydraulic, and very similar to an F1 car's, in that it uses a mechanical spring to sense the amount of torque the driver is putting in, before opening a hydraulic valve to feed fluid either way. The ceramic front brake discs are 390mm diameter, the rears 380mm.

"The great thing about this is it's very similar to F1 but over a longer time scale," Newey says. "An F1 car is 12–18 months in development before it goes to the first test. Work on the RB17 started in Christmas 2020 and we've been in the concept phase for three years or more. That's allowed us to really quiz it, be self-critical, be careful on the direction we've taken, go off on a route, evaluated it, and changed to another."

It's not something they usually have the luxury of doing, Newey adds, and the upshot is that this is pretty much the third generation of the car before the first one has even appeared. "It's had three different engines, it started off being all-wheel drive, with the e-motor on the front axle rather than the rear, until our simulations showed it was better to be rear drive, once you're free of a weight limit. I was happy

"PRODUCTION IS LIMITED TO 50 CARS AND THEY'LL BE MADE AT RED BULL'S TECH CAMPUS"

about that. Rear drive is easier to manage," he says, before confirming the car you see here is still not fully signed off. His team are a patient lot.

Work on the interior is ongoing, although the seating configuration was frozen early on. "That was all part of the basic package. The available structural space is now fixed, and we're working on the ergonomics, where we put the screens and switchgear. The interior is an important factor. We don't want it to be a spartan race car cabin. Physical buttons, definitely, especially on a car with this level of performance. You need a physical knob you can change. Then there will be interior options." Massage seats? "It's the car," Newey says, without missing a beat. (We were joking.)

The powertrain will be on the dyno by the time you read this, with development work gathering pace throughout 2024. All the sub systems will have been proven out before coming together in the first few test cars, ahead of a track debut in summer 2025. Production is limited to 50 cars, all of which will be made at Red Bull's ever-expanding technology campus near Milton Keynes. The manufacturing processes mirror those of an F1 car, another thing that underpins the RB17's unique selling proposition. An accessible one that still generates unparalleled excitement.

The RB17 enters an unusual and stratospheric part of the automotive world. The normal rules don't apply; in fact, there are no rules at all, which is part of the allure. Ferrari's XX programme is now well established, and the Prancing Horse recently added the 499P Modificata for rich mortals to play with alongside its amazing F1 Corse Clienti programme. But the RB17 exists in its own world, a clean sheet design from one of the undoubted masters of the motorsport universe, pushing the boundaries once again.

"Some people haven't really understood the Valkyrie," Newey muses, as calmly understated as ever. "You can buy a Honda Goldwing and get one experience or a modern superbike and get a very different experience. The Valkyrie is clearly at the superbike end of things. The RB17 is the next level on, several levels to be honest, from that in terms of its performance. Yes, of course if you get in half asleep and not focused it has the potential to bite. If you get in with that tingle of adrenalin and nervousness, I think that's part of the excitement."

The equations got Red Bull to this point. The rest is pure rock'n'roll.

WHY IT'S HERE
Going fully electric means that horsepower and handling are an order of magnitude greater. But does the car have *soul*?

RIMAC NEVERA

The software guys, Miro had advised with a smile, aren't human. The Croatians, you quickly learn, are a nation of plain speakers. Even about their own co-workers. Miro Zrnčević is Rimac's Chief Test Driver, a big, bluff guy who loves cars and has one of the key tasks on the company's Nevera hypercar: locating the soul of a machine whose colossal abilities are corralled by a frenzy of ones and zeroes, like the discombobulating opening credits of *The Matrix*.

This has sent him on a journey of discovery in parallel with the software guys. "It's very strange," he ponders, "because during development I would drive the car and give them feedback. They would stare at the data on their laptops and say, 'is this better?' And it would be, despite the fact that they have never even driven the car."

Better here takes on a wholly different meaning. Better here means ballistic. Or brain-scrambling. Welcome to hypercar v2.0, a world where everything you know about very (very) fast cars has changed forever. Sure, software has long played a role in setting parameters but never as profoundly as this. The Nevera's topline numbers game is seriously strong. Only 150 will be made, costing £1.7m each (plus local taxes). It accelerates to 62mph in 1.81 seconds, demolishes the quarter mile from a standing start in 8.25 and eclipses 186mph in 9.23 seconds. This makes the Nevera marginally faster even than a contemporary Formula One car. Sheesh. Consider that it weighs 2,300kg – 700 of which consists of the battery pack – and you get some idea how utterly nuts the physics are here.

Rimac doubled down on the Nevera's performance potential when it established or smashed a stack of world performance records in 2023 (23 in one day, in fact). This included setting a 0–249mph time of 29.93 seconds. Crazier still, youthful test driver Goran Drndak managed 171.34mph in *reverse*. Then again, we're well acquainted with the crazy accelerative feats of the most powerful EVs. It's one of the things these cars can just do. What really matters is if this electric car goes beyond the cerebral and scientific to generate the sort of visceral response you get when a V12 ticks past 8,000rpm in third gear and rips the air asunder. That's just as tricky.

How does it feel when you first climb aboard? Mate Rimac, the main man, wanted a car that was easy to use and live with, a car with a GT aspect to it despite its vast power reserves. So the butterfly doors eat helpfully into the roof and you don't need to be an elastic gymnast to get in and out. The view ahead is useful thanks to visible, curvy front wings, and the car is easy to place on the road. This really counts for a lot on the move. And when you pull those doors shut they close with a resounding, expensively damped whump.

Watch the Nevera on the move and the more you appreciate the nuances and subtleties of its shape. It has a strong sense of theatre but it's closer to the Honda NSX than a Ferrari SF90. It's not generic but there's a certain

The Nevera's cabin uses almost exclusively bespoke components. Only the heating and ventilation system is borrowed (from the Audi R8). This is a hyper-GT, so it's designed to be comfortable and user-friendly. The various drive modes are activated via a rotary controller

Left, for an EV start up, Rimac has gone to extraordinary lengths. You would expect an electric hypercar to be data-driven, but they've even devised their own type-faces

Left, for a country with zero experience in car manufacture, Rimac has got off to a deeply impressive start

The Rimac Nevera is a car of great ambition but, despite the company's relative inexperience, it has created something seismic. This is the poster car for a new generation of car fans, electro- rather than petrolheads

familiarity to the form language, the shape largely dictated by aerodynamic and cooling requirements, including Rimac's signature "cravat" motif ahead of the rear wheelarch. "The neck-tie has provided a symbol of Croatian strength and identity since the 17th century," says the company's charming Design Director, Adriano Mudri. So now you know.

Everything inside bar the Audi R8-sourced HVAC is home-grown, from the main infotainment system and all its software to the interior door handles, switchgear and air vents, which are made from billet aluminium. The steering wheel feels great and the indicators are Ferrari-like buttons. Column stalks aren't very Rimac-y and surely it's only a matter of time before we're "thinking" our indicators on and off. There are three hi-definition TFT screens, running bespoke software and graphics. The main one is configurable, displaying all the info you need plus some stuff you probably don't: there's a real time torque display, which shows how much each wheel is coping with, a g-meter, and various other read-outs that are difficult to process on the move. The central screen handles infotainment, phone, navigation, climate control but it's also where you go to adjust the seats. You get used to it but a simple manual adjustment would be much easier.

The Nevera's architecture encompasses a 6,960-cell, 120kWh Lithium/Manganese/Nickel battery pack in an H shape along the spine and behind the cockpit. There are four surface-mounted permanent magnet motors driving each wheel individually, the most advanced torque vectoring ever achieved, a power output equivalent to 1,889bhp and 1,740 lb ft of torque. A pair of single-speed gearboxes are connected to the front wheels, and there are two at the rear in one housing. The Nevera has a range of 303 miles WLTP, and hooked up to a 500 kW charger takes 19 minutes to go from zero to an 80 per cent state of charge.

Yet there's no future shock to the Nevera in everyday use. The drive controller is a rotary dial to the left of the steering wheel that you push to wake everything up, then scroll through P, R, N and D. When we drove a prototype, the dial was glitchy and fiddly to use, but a later production car we were fortunate enough to have for 350 miles in a single (very memorable) day had a haptic as expensive-feeling as a piece of haute horologie.

Squeeze the Nevera's throttle and the resulting torrent of energy is like lava erupting from a volcano. Even a big multi-cylindered combustion engine takes a beat or two to get its act together but the Rimac just warps forward. That idea of "thinking" your indicators on and off: well this is thought or intention instantly made real. Nothing accelerates with such vigour or judiciously managed force. It is utterly extraordinary.

Let's just explode a myth here, though: fast cars aren't all about simply going fast. The how, why and what happens along the way is what colours in the space between. The Nevera's fully electric steering is well calibrated and allows you to pour the car in and out of corners with a linear motion. It's not overflowing with natural feel but then "feel" is a dark art these days. There are seven different drive modes on offer, 'Sport' being the optimum if you're after the most rounded everyday drive, by way of sharpened throttle, brakes, suspension and steering. 'Range' is obviously leaner with the energy, 'Track' turns everything up to 11, 'Custom' allows you to mix and match, while 'Drift' basically sends all the torque to the rear axle if you want to bonfire your huge and expensive Michelin Pilot Sports (275/35 up front, 315/35 at the rear).

Drive it in one of its less aggressive modes and the Nevera does a very reasonable impression of, say, a Bentley Continental GT. It's suspended on double wishbones all round with electronically controlled dampers and active ride height, so it's tolerably comfortable at everyday speeds, if occasionally crashy over sudden surface imperfections. Honestly, plenty of sports saloons on big wheels are far more uncouth.

This really is a car with a multi-layered personality. The secret sauce here, of course, is the torque vectoring, a fiendishly complex set-up that effectively turns the Rimac into five cars in one. There are 77 separate ECUs and millions of lines of code hustling around its body – mainframe? – but rather than schizophrenia, the result is a remarkable bandwidth. The Rimac All-Wheel Torque Vectoring (R-AWTV 2) effectively supplants regular ESP

"FEW CARS ACCELERATE WITH SUCH VIGOUR OR CAREFULLY MANAGED FORCE"

Not a gamechanger in terms of how it looks, the Rimac Nevera nonetheless ushers in the new electric breed in phenomenal style

and traction control systems, working predictively and responsively to make 100 calculations per second. Depending on mode, you can revel in all-wheel grip, neutralising understeer and finding a friendly balance, or send all the torque to the rear axle and do daft skids all day long.

In 'Sport' mode, the Nevera summons up the wieldiness you'd find in, say, the Porsche 911 Turbo but punches out of a corner with the ferocity of something that has three times the Porsche's horsepower (which it has). This hurricane force isn't a surprise but its agility and poise are really something. As is the way it sloughs off its mass: it feels half a tonne lighter than it is, like a car with optimal weight distribution and centre of gravity rather than one with a Caterham Seven's worth of battery at its heart. Sometimes this can catch you out, such are the immutable laws of physics.

And it has authentic brake feel, so often an EV issue. An electro-hydraulic brake booster with a pedal feel simulator distributes braking force between the friction brakes – beefy 390mm Brembo carbon ceramics front and rear – and the electric powertrain, depending on which is thermally optimal. The Nevera offers the highest amount of regenerative braking of any EV currently on sale, and you can hustle effectively along a twisty road in one-pedal mode. The faster you go, the bigger the leap of faith.

Then there's the Nevera's chassis, made entirely of carbon fibre – bonded roof, integrated battery housing and rear subframe – which gives it the torsional rigidity of an LMP car. Rimac claims it's the most rigid road car ever made, and at 70,000 Nm/degree, an order of magnitude stiffer even than the structurally superb Lamborghini Revuelto. There's the odd creak and groan – carbon fibre can generate unusual acoustic anomalies – but mostly you're just aware of how phenomenally well engineered the Nevera is. Yes, the urge remains to reach for shift paddles, and the seamless nature of the powertrain invariably removes a layer of interaction. It simply doesn't sizzle like a V12. But as you can imagine, the availability of almost 2,000 expertly calibrated horsepower compensates. And actually it sounds really good, an authentic mix of whoosh, whir and sci-fi. Not so far from a Bugatti Chiron, then. And faster. Difficult to compute, that.

Of course, you really need an empty runway to experience the full madness. Performing a launch start is dead easy: select 'Track' mode on the dash-mounted rotary controller nearest your

SPECIFICATION

TECH
NEVERA HAS 77 SEPARATE ECUS AND MILLIONS OF LINES OF CODE... TORQUE VECTORING REPLACES ESP

CHASSIS
MADE ENTIRELY OF CARBON FIBRE, NEVERA IS THE MOST RIGID ROAD CAR EVER MADE, FEELS SUPER STIFF ON THE MOVE

POWERTRAIN
120KWH BATTERY PACK SITS IN AN H SHAPE ALONG THE SPINE AND BEHIND THE COCKPIT. TOTAL OUTPUT IS 1,877BHP

BRAKES
NEVERA OFFERS THE HIGHEST AMOUNT OF REGEN BRAKING OF ANY CAR, AND WORKS WELL IN ONE-PEDAL MODE MOST OF THE TIME

VEHICLE TYPE –
FULLY ELECTRIC, ALL-WHEEL DRIVE COUPE

POWERTRAIN –
FOUR INDEPENDENT SURFACE-MOUNTED, PERMANENT-MAGNET ELECTRIC MOTORS, WITH INDEPENDENT INVERTERS AND GEARBOXES, ALL-WHEEL DRIVE WITH TORQUE VECTORING. FRONT MOTORS 303BHP AND 199LB FT EACH, REAR MOTORS 603BHP AND 663LB FT EACH; TOTAL SYSTEM OUTPUT 1,877BHP; 120KWH LITHIUM MANGANESE NICKEL BATTERY PACK

WEIGHT: 2,300KG (DRY)

DIMENSIONS –
LENGTH: 4,724MM
WIDTH: 2,049MM
HEIGHT: 1,240MM

TRANSMISSION –
TWO SINGLE SPEED GEARBOXES AT THE FRONT, TWO SINGLE GEARBOXES AT THE REAR IN ONE HOUSING

PERFORMANCE –
TOP SPEED 258MPH
0–62MPH 1.81 SECONDS
0–186MPH 9.23 SECONDS
RANGE: 303 MILES

BRAIN-FRAZZLING FACT:

ON THE SAME DAY IN MAY 2023, RIMAC SET 23 DIFFERENT PERFORMANCE RECORDS, INCLUDING 0-249MPH IN 29.93 SECONDS, 124-186MPH IN 4.79 SECONDS, AND A STANDING MILE IN 20.59 SECONDS. LATER THAT YEAR, THE COMPANY BROKE ANOTHER GUINNESS WORLD RECORD WHEN TEST DRIVER GORAN DRNDAK DROVE A NEVERA AT 171.34MPH – IN REVERSE.

"THE CENTRAL SCREEN IS ALSO HOME TO THE NEVERA'S TELEMETRY, WHICH CAN BE DOWNLOADED AND ANALYSED LATER ON"

right hand, press the brake for a few seconds, then release and stand on the accelerator. The next 10 or 15 seconds are simply vaporised. Time ceases to exist, or at least exist in the form in which we normally recognise it. Whatever happens, it's worth doing twice just to be sure. Then a third time to double-check that what happened the first two times was for real. By this point your internal organs will have swapped places, a situation that a spell exploring the Drift mode does little to help. It's the strangest sensation.

Mate Rimac is a self-confessed data fiend so the central screen is also home to the Nevera's telemetry, which can be downloaded to a laptop or smartphone for review. He meets us at our runway, sitting under a gazebo, looking curious but beneficent. Once he's happy that we're happy, he gleefully demonstrates where the acceleration was most vigorous, the mode we used, and how much power was expended: 1,580bhp apparently. Not so much Big Brother as your genius Croatian cousin.

Rimac has developed its own M2M data system to allow owners to analyse driving performance, metrics and map previews on all the usual platforms. And of course over-the-air updates are available, as is the way with the new electric order. On top of all this, there's also an AI driver coach, which uses the car's 12 ultrasonic sensors, 13 cameras and 6 radar hooked up to the latest NVIDIA Pegasus operating system to overlay race circuits in real-time to allow drivers to work on the perfect line, as well as braking and acceleration points.

There's a lot to unpack here. As the first true pure-electric hypercar to land, there's a pioneering feel to the Rimac Nevera. This thing's quarter mile time absolutely blitzes the Bugatti Chiron Sport's and its pace everywhere is intergalactic. But the most powerful ICE cars also generate huge character, and it's their engines and the noise they make that tend to linger longest in the memory. Even the highest of high performance can become one-dimensional after a while.

Yet the Nevera feels like a car that's been engineered and developed by people who aren't just way ahead of the technological and software curve, they have an innate feeling for the hardware too. Put all the elements together and you have a car that isn't just entertaining, it also feels like a significant step on the road ahead. Think of Rimac as a sort of techno Pagani, with as much focus on artistry as artificial intelligence. Turns out that those software dudes are human after all.

Right, data nerds will not run out of things to analyse on the Nevera. Below, butterfly doors are the main concession to hypercar styling

CREDITS

PHOTOGRAPHERS:

TOM BARNES, DAVE BURNETT, JONATHAN FLEETWOOD, MARK FAGELSON, WILSON HENNESSY, ALEX HOWE, DENNIS NOTEN, MARK RICCIONI, PHILIPP RUPPRECHT, JOHN WYCHERLEY

WRITERS:

JASON BARLOW, CHRIS HARRIS, OLIVER MARRIAGE, JACK RIX

REPROGRAPHIC AND CGI:

MAGIC TORCH, AMAR KAKAD, BEFUNKY.COM

WITH THANKS TO:

PHOEBE LINDSLEY, ESTHER NEVE, ELLIOTT WEBB, OLLIE KEW, PAUL HORRELL, ROWAN HORNCASTLE, TOM FORD, VIJAY PATTNI, BEN PULMAN AND THE *TOP GEAR* EDITORIAL TEAM, CHARLIE TURNER, FLAVIO MANZONI, MITJA BORKERT, SIMON SPROULE, ADRIAN NEWEY, ROB GRAY, RACHAEL LAWSON, HORACIO PAGANI, SEBASTIAN BERRIDI, GORDON MURRAY, SARAH SMITH

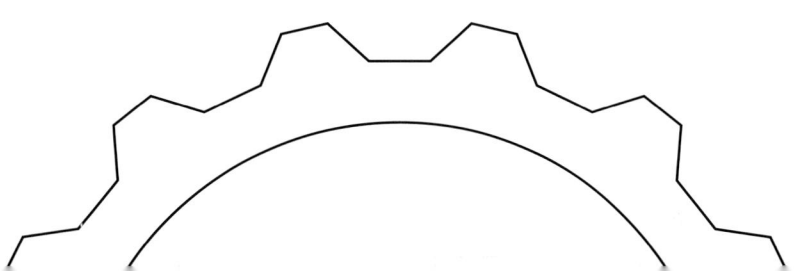

BBC Books, an imprint of Ebury Publishing
One Embassy Gardens, 8 Viaduct Gdns,
Nine Elms, London SW11 7BW

BBC Books is part of the Penguin Random House group of companies whose addresses can be found at global.penguinrandomhouse.com

Main text by **Jason Barlow**
Text Copyright © *Top Gear* Magazine 2024
Image Copyright © *Top Gear* Magazine

BBC, TOP GEAR and THE STIG (word marks and logos) are trademarks of the British Broadcasting Corporation and are used under licence. BBC logo © BBC 1996.
Top Gear logo © BBC 2005. Licensed by BBC Studios

Jason Barlow has asserted his right to be identified as the author of this Work in accordance with the Copyright, Designs and Patents Act 1988

First published by BBC Books in 2024

www.penguin.co.uk

A CIP catalogue record for this book is available from the British Library

ISBN 9781785948022

Editor: **Phoebe Lindsley**
Design: **Andy Franklin**
Production: **Phil Spencer**

Printed and bound in Italy by Printer Trento

No part of this book may be used or reproduced in any manner for the purpose of training artificial intelligence technologies or systems. In accordance with Article 4(3) of the DSM Directive 2019/790, Penguin Random House expressly reserves this work from the text and data mining exception.

The authorised representative in the EEA is Penguin Random House Ireland, Morrison Chambers, 32 Nassau Street, Dublin D02 YH68.

Penguin Random House is committed to a sustainable future for our business, our readers and our planet. This book is made from Forest Stewardship Council® certified paper.